Nick Vandome

Android Phones
for Seniors

3rd edition
Illustrated using Android 10

In easy steps is an imprint of In Easy Steps Limited
16 Hamilton Terrace · Holly Walk · Leamington Spa
Warwickshire · United Kingdom · CV32 4LY
www.ineasysteps.com

Third Edition

In Easy Steps Limited supports The Forest Stewardship Council (FSC),
the leading international forest certification organization. All our titles
that are printed on Greenpeace approved FSC certified paper carry the
FSC logo.

MIX
Paper from
responsible sources
FSC® C020837

Printed and bound in the United Kingdom

ISBN 978-1-84078-942-3

Contents

4   Around an Android Phone   55

5   Calls and Contacts   79

1 Introducing Android Phones

Smartphones using the Android operating system are the most used phones worldwide. This chapter gives an overview of Android on a smartphone. It also looks at creating a Google Account for using Google services on your Android phone.

About Android

Android is essentially a mobile computing operating system – i.e. one for mobile devices such as smartphones and tablets.

Android is an open source operating system, which means that the source code is made available to hardware manufacturers and developers so that they can design their devices and apps in conjunction with Android. This has created a large community of Android developers, and also means that Android is not tied to one specific device; individual manufacturers can use it (as long as they meet certain specific criteria), which has led to Android being available on a variety of different devices.

Android Inc. was founded in 2003, and the eponymous operating system was initially developed for mobile devices. Google quickly saw this as an opportunity to enter the smartphone and tablet market and bought Android in 2005. The first Android-powered smartphone appeared in 2008 and since then has gone from strength to strength. Android-based smartphones have a majority of the worldwide market, and it is used by numerous manufacturers on their handsets.

The main differences between the Android mobile operating system and desktop- or laptop-based ones such as Windows or macOS are:

- **No file structure**. There is no default built-in file manager structure for storing and managing files. All content is saved within the app in which it is created.

- **Self-contained apps**. Because there is no file structure, apps are generally self-contained and do not communicate with each other, unless required.

- **Numerous Home screens**. There are numerous Home screens on an Android phone, and they can be used to store and access apps.

- Generally, **content is saved automatically as it is created**. Apps save content as it is created, so there is no Save or Save As function within many apps.

Android is based on the flexible and robust Linux operating system and shares many similarities with it.

The New icon pictured above indicates a new or enhanced feature introduced with Android phones using Android 10.

About Android Phones

Android has been used on smartphones since 2008. Initially adoption was fairly slow, but this has now accelerated to the point where Android is the most widely used operating system on smartphones.

Combinations of Android phones

Since Android can be used by different manufacturers, this means that a range of the latest smartphones always run on Android. In addition, since not all older phones are designed to be upgraded to the latest version of Android, there are phones running several different versions of Android – for instance, the Google Pixel 6 runs the latest version of Android (at the time of printing, Android 12), while some models of older phones may still only be able to run Android 6.0 Marshmallow. As a result, there are hundreds of combinations in terms of smartphone models and versions of Android on the market. Some are the expensive flagship models, which will run a relatively new version of Android (although not necessarily the very latest version) compared with cheaper models that can only run an older version of Android.

Checking for versions of Android

When buying an Android phone, look at the version of Android in the phone's specification. Ideally, it should be a relatively new version, in order to enable it to be upgraded to the latest version when it becomes available. Some models of Android phones reach a point where they do not have the required hardware to update to the next version of Android and are therefore stuck with the current version that they are using. This may also limit the phone's ability to download and use the latest apps that are available.

Android phone differences

Despite the variations in versions of Android, the user experience is generally the same on different Android phones. However, one area of difference is in the hardware used by manufacturers. For instance, some newer Android phones have fingerprint sensors for unlocking the phone, and others have more sophisticated cameras.

Updated versions of Android were historically named alphabetically after items of confectionery but are now named numerically.

Due to the range of versions of Android on smartphones, it is not feasible to cover all possibilities across different manufacturers. Therefore, this book will focus on the standard functionality of Android that is available through all versions of the operating system. It will feature Android version 10, which is the version of Android most widely adopted on Android phones (at the time of printing). The examples will also be from a Samsung phone, one of the most widely used brands of smartphone on the market.

Updating Android

Since Android is open source and can be used on a variety of different devices, this can sometimes cause delays in updating the operating system on the full range of eligible Android devices. This is because it has to be tailored specifically for each different device; it is not a case of "one size fits all". This can lead to delays in the latest version being rolled out to all compatible devices. The product cycle for new versions is usually six to nine months.

As Android is a Google product, Google's own devices are usually the first ones to run the latest version of the software. Therefore, the Google Pixel 6 was the first phone to run the latest version of Android, 12, while others are still running previous versions, such as 6.0 Marshmallow, 7.0 Nougat, 8.0 Oreo and 9, 10 and 11. For recently released phones, an upgrade to the latest version of Android will be scheduled into the update calendar or it might be already available to install. However, for some older Android phones the latest version of the software is not always made available. This can be because of hardware limitations, but there have also been suggestions that it is a move by hardware manufacturers designed to ensure that consumers upgrade to the latest products.

The version of the Android operating system that is being used on your phone can be viewed from within the **Software update** section of the **Settings** app. This is where details of the current version of Android can be viewed.

Much of the general functionality of the Android operating system is the same, regardless of the version being used.

For more details about Android settings, see Chapter 3.

< Software update   Q

Download and install
Last checked on: November 22, 2021
Downloading via mobile networks may result in additional charges. If possible, download via a Wi-Fi network instead.

Auto download over Wi-Fi
Download software updates automatically when connected to a Wi-Fi network.

Last update
The last update was installed on November 22, 2021 at 14:45.

Settings

Android Overlays

Because Android is an open source operating system, it means that manufacturers can amend it, to a certain extent, when they add it to their phone models. This keeps the core Android operating system, but the user interface can be adapted so that it becomes specific to each manufacturer. This is known as an "overlay" and means that the appearance of Android will be different on, for instance, a Samsung phone and an HTC one. However, the operation of Android will still be the same on different brands of phones and, in most cases, the appearance of the user interface will be very similar and still recognizable as Android.

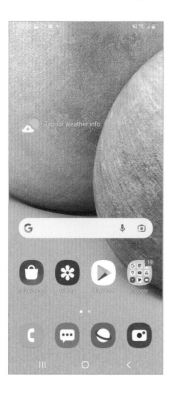

If you are familiar with one brand of Android phone and then switch to another, it may take a little while to get used to the overlay of the new phone. However, the underlying functionality should be the same.

In addition to overlays, manufacturers can also add their own apps to their brand of Android phone and, in some cases, have their own app store for downloading more apps.

The one phone that does not have any kind of overlay is the Google Pixel 6: since Google own Android, they use the operating system in its purest form on their phones.

Features of Android 10

Although Android 11 and 12 are both newer versions than 10, they are only available on a limited number of Android phones, and version 10 has a higher adoption rate. The majority of features are the same as for earlier versions of Android. However, there are also some new Android 10 features.

The features on these two pages are all updates from previous versions of Android.

Gestures navigation

This can be applied to use gestures on the screen for certain operations, rather than just using the controls and the buttons on the device. To use gestures:

1 Tap on the **Settings** app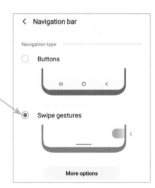

2 Tap on the **Display** option

Display
Brightness, Blue light filter, Home screen

3 Tap on the **Navigation bar** option

Navigation bar
Manage the Home, Back, and Recents buttons or use gestures for more screen space.

Beware

If **Swipe gestures** is turned **On**, the control buttons at the bottom of the Android phone will not be available.

4 Tap **On** the **Swipe gestures** button

< Navigation bar

Navigation type

○ Buttons

III   O   <

◉ Swipe gestures

More options

5 The navigation bar is displayed at the bottom  of the screen. Use this to apply gestures – e.g. swipe up on it to return to the Home screen from any app

Dark Mode

This enables the screen colors to be changed so that they are dark, with the other elements becoming light; essentially, the screen colors are inverted. To use Dark Mode:

1 Tap on the **Settings** app

2 Tap on the **Display** tab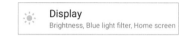

3 In the Display settings, tap on the **Dark** button to activate Dark Mode on the Android phone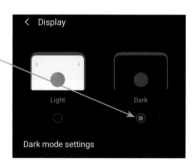

Focus mode

This can be used to turn off specific apps and notifications so that you can concentrate on tasks without being interrupted. To use Focus mode:

1 Tap on the **Settings** app

2 Tap on the **Digital Wellbeing and parental controls** tab

3 Tap on one of the **Focus mode** options to set the required specifics for the Focus – i.e. which apps are allowed and how notifications are dealt with

For more details about using the **Digital Wellbeing and parental controls** settings, see pages 182-185.

Features of Android Phones

The button for turning a phone on and off is located on the side of the body of the device in most cases, as are the other buttons and ports that can be used for various functions on your phone.

On/Off button

This can also be used to put the phone into Sleep mode. Press and hold for a couple of seconds to turn on the phone. Press once to put it to sleep or wake it up from sleep.

Don't forget

If the Android operating system is updated on a phone, it will probably restart before the update takes effect.

Turning off

To turn off an Android phone, press and hold on the **On/Off** button until the **Power off** button appears on the screen. Tap on this to turn the phone off. Tap on **Restart** to shut down the phone and then start it again.

Volume button

This is either a single button on the opposite side to the **On/Off** button or two separate buttons. Press the buttons to adjust the volume.

Cameras

There is the main, rear-facing camera (on the back of the phone) for taking pictures. Most phones also have a front-facing camera (on the screen side of the phone), which is usually a lower resolution and is useful for making video calls or taking "selfies", as the user can view the screen at the same time as using the camera.

"Selfies" are photos taken of yourself, using the front-facing camera (on the screen of the phone).

Headphone jack

This is used to connect a headphone cable, and is usually at the top or bottom of the phone.

Micro USB port

This can be used to attach the phone to an adapter for charging the phone, or to a computer for charging or to download content from (or upload to) the phone, using the supplied USB cable. Once the phone is connected to a computer it will show up as a removable drive in the file manager, in the same way as an item such as a flashdrive.

An increasing number of phones, particularly the higher-end models, have a fingerprint sensor on the body of the phone that can be used to unlock the phone with a unique fingerprint. Fingerprint sensors have to be set up by using the applicable item (usually in the **Settings** app) and then pressing on the sensor several times so that it can identify your unique fingerprint. More than one fingerprint can usually be set up for use with the sensor.

microSD cards

These can be inserted into the appropriate slot on the body of the phone to increase the amount of storage for items such as photos and music.

SIM Cards

The SIM card for your Android phone will be provided by your mobile carrier – i.e. the company that provides your cellular phone and data services. Without this, you would still be able to communicate using your phone, but only via Wi-Fi and compatible services. A SIM card gives you access to a mobile network too. Newer Android phones have a slot on the side (a SIM tray) for inserting a SIM card. To insert a SIM card into the side SIM tray:

SIM cards usually use 3G, 4G or 5G networks for providing cellular phone and data services – e.g. texting and messaging. 5G is the fastest, but is not currently as widely available as 3G and 4G. The G in the name stands for Generation.

16

Some Android phones, particularly older models, have the SIM tray located inside the phone, and this can be accessed by removing the back panel of the phone. The battery can also be located here in Android phones where the SIM is accessed in this way.

1 The SIM tray is located on the side of the phone, with a small hole at the end of it

2 Use the SIM tool (which should be provided with the phone) to open the SIM tray, by pressing firmly into the hole shown in Step 1

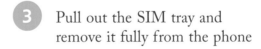

3 Pull out the SIM tray and remove it fully from the phone

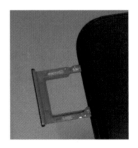

4 Insert the SIM card into the SIM tray and return it into the slot in the phone. (Some SIM trays have compartments for different sizes of SIM cards)

Setting Up Your Phone

When you first turn on your phone (by pressing and holding the **On/Off** button) you will be taken through the setup process. This only has to be done once, and some of the steps can be completed or amended at a later time, usually within the **Settings** app. Some of the elements that can be applied during the setup process include:

- **Language**. This option lets you select the language to use for your phone. Whichever language is selected will affect all of the system text on the phone, and it will also apply to all user accounts on the phone.

- **Wi-Fi**. This can be used to set up your Wi-Fi so that you can access web and online services. In the **Select Wi-Fi** window, tap on the name of your router. Enter the password for your router and tap on the **Connect** button.

- **Google Account**. At this stage, you can create a Google Account or sign in with an existing one. Once you have done this, you will have full access to the Google Account services and you will not have to enter your login details again. (A Google Account can also be set up at a later time; see pages 20-21.)

- **Google services**. This includes options for which of the Google services you want to use, including backing up your phone, using location services, and sending feedback to Google.

- **Date and time**. This can be used to set the date and time, either manually or automatically.

- **Method of screen lock**. This can be used to set a lock for the phone, using a fingerprint, PIN code, pattern or a password.

- **Screen layout**. This can be used to create a larger interface on the phone's screen, by changing the size of the items on it and the font size.

Most routers require a password when they are accessed for the first time by a new device. This is a security measure to ensure that other people cannot gain unauthorized access to your router and Wi-Fi.

The Wi-Fi has to be connected in order for a Google Account to be created or signed in to during the setting up of the phone.

Since Android is owned by Google, much of its functionality is provided through a Google Account.

Don't forget

If you already have a Gmail Account, this will also serve as your Google Account, and the login details (email address and password) can be used for both.

Google TV is a new feature with Android 10.

Don't forget

When you buy anything through your Google Account, such as music, apps or movies, you will have to enter your credit or debit card details (unless you are downloading a free app), which will be used for future purchases through your Google Account.

Android and Google

Most phones are linked to specific companies for the provision of their services and selection of apps: Apple for the iPhone and Google for phones using Android, as well as the phone's manufacturer (e.g. Samsung). As with the other phones, for Android phones you must have a linked account to get the most out of your phone. This is a Google Account, and is created free of charge with a Google email address (Gmail) and a password. Once it has been created, your Google Account will give you access to a number of built-in Android apps and also additional services such as backing up and storing your content online.

When you first set up your phone, you can enter your Google Account details or select to create a new account. You can also do this at any time by accessing one of the apps that requires access to a Google Account. These include:

- **Play Store**, for obtaining more apps.
- **Google TV**, for obtaining movies and TV shows.
- **Play Books**, for obtaining books.
- **Google News** app for displaying news stories.

When you access one of these apps you will be prompted to create a Google Account. You do not have to do so at this point, but it will give you access to the full range of Google Account services.

Other apps such as the **Photos** app for storing and viewing photos can be used on their own, but if a Google Account has been set up, the content can be backed up automatically.

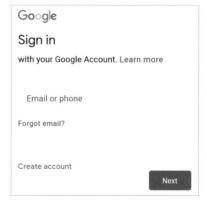

Some of the benefits of a Google Account include:

- Access from any computer or mobile device with web access, from the **accounts.google.com/** page.
Once you have entered your account details you can access online Google services, including Calendar, Gmail and the Play Store.

- Keep your content synchronized and backed up. With a Google Account, all of your linked data will be automatically synchronized so that it is available for all web-enabled devices, and it will also be backed up by the Google servers.

If you buy items from the Play Store through your Google Account on the web, they will also be available on your Android phone.

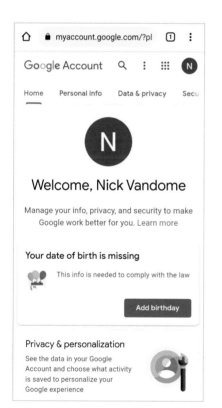

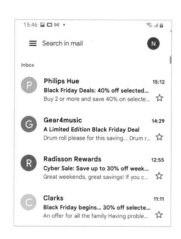

A new Google Account can also be created within **Settings** > **Accounts and backup** > **Accounts** on your phone. Tap on the **Add account** button and tap on the **Google** button. Then, enter the required details for the new Google Account (see pages 20-21).

19

- Peace of mind that your content is protected. There is a **Security** section on your Google Account web page where you can apply various security settings and alerts.

Creating a Google Account

A new Google Account can be created in the following different ways:

- During the initial setup of your Android phone.

- When you first access one of the relevant apps, as explained on page 18.

- From the **Settings** app, by selecting **Accounts and backup** > **Accounts** > **Add account**.

For each of the above, the process for creating a Google Account is the same.

Don't forget

During the account setup process there is also a screen for account recovery, where you can add an answer to a question so that your account details can be retrieved by Google if you forget them.

1 If you already have an account, enter your sign-in details, or tap on the **Create account** option

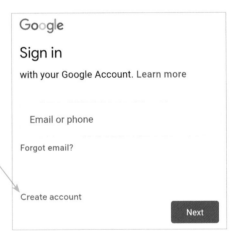

2 Enter the first and last name for the new account user, then tap on the **Next** button

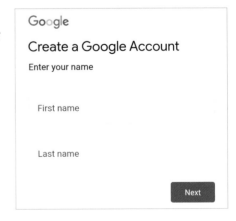

3 Enter a username (this will also become your Gmail address), then tap on the **Next** button at the bottom of the screen

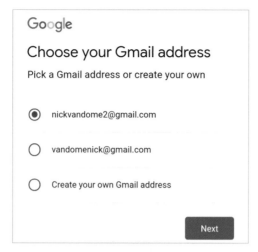

A username for a Google Account is a unique name created by the user, which is suffixed by *@gmail.com*.

4 Create a password for the account and then re-enter it for confirmation. Tap on the **Next** button at the bottom of the screen

If your chosen username has already been taken, you will be prompted to amend it. This can usually be done by adding a sequence of numbers to the end of it, but make sure you remember the sequence correctly.

5 The account details are displayed. Tap on the **Next** button to sign in with your new account

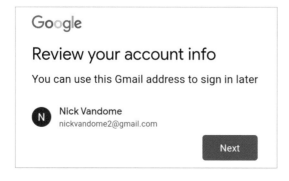

21

Using a Touchscreen

The traditional method of interacting with a computer is by using a mouse and a keyboard as the input devices. However, this has all changed with smartphones; they are much more tactile devices that are controlled by tapping and swiping on the touchscreen. This activates and controls the apps and settings on the phone, and enables you to add content with the virtual keyboard that appears at appropriate times.

Gently does it

Touchscreens are sensitive devices and only require a light touch to activate the required command. To get the best out of your touchscreen:

- Tap, swipe or press gently on the screen. Do not use excessive force and do not keep tapping with increasing pressure if something does not work in the way in which you expected. Instead, try performing another action and then returning to the original one.

- Tap with your fingertip rather than your fingernail. This will be more effective in terms of performing the required operation, and is better for the surface of the touchscreen.

- For the majority of touchscreen tasks, tap, press or swipe at one point on the screen. The exception to this is zooming in and out on certain items (such as web pages), which can be done by swiping outward and pinching inward with thumb and forefinger.

- Keep your touchscreen dry, and make sure that your fingers are also clean and free of moisture.

- Use a cover to protect the screen when not in use, particularly if you are carrying your phone in a jacket pocket or a bag.

- Use a screen cloth to keep the screen clean and free of fingerprints and smears. The touchscreen should still work if it has fingerprints and marks on it, but it will become harder to see clearly what is on the screen.

Hot tip

If you are using your phone in an area where there is likely to be moisture, such as in the kitchen if you are following a recipe, cover the touchscreen in some form of light plastic wrap to protect it from any spills or splashes.

...cont'd

Touchscreen controls

Touchscreens can be controlled with three main types of actions. These are:

- **Tapping**. Tap once on an item such as an app to activate it. This can also be used for the main navigation control buttons at the bottom of the touchscreen, or for items such as **On/Off** buttons when applying settings for specific items.

For more information about working with apps on the Home screen and the Notification panel, see Chapter 4.

- **Pressing**. Press and hold on an item on the Home screen to move its position or place it in the **Favorites Tray** at the bottom of the screen.

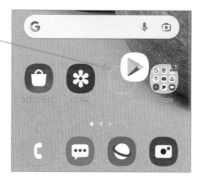

- **Swiping**. Swipe down from the top of the Home screen to access the **Notification panel** and the **Quick Settings**, and swipe left and right to view all of the available Home screens, or to scroll through photo albums.

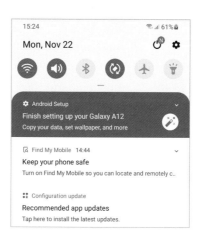

Using Apps

One of the great selling points for Android phones is the range of apps that are available for them. At the time of printing, there are at least 3.4 million Android apps in the Google Play Store, with others available from third-party developers. Some are free, while others are paid for.

The built-in apps are the ones that give the initial functionality to your phone, and include items such as email, a web browser, a calendar, a calculator and maps. They appear as icons on your phone's Home screen or in the **All Apps** area (see page 56), and are accessed by tapping on them once.

Managing apps

When you switch from one app to another you do not have to close down the original one that you were using. Android keeps it running in the background, but in a state of hibernation so that it is not using up any memory or processing power on your phone. To do this:

1. Tap on an app to open it and move through its screens as required. Tap on the **Home** button on the phone's Navigation bar at the bottom of the screen to return to the Home screen at any point. The app will remain open in the background

2. Tap on the app again. It will open up at the point at which you left it

You can also move back to the Home screen by tapping on the **Back** button. This takes you back through the screens that you have accessed within the app, until you reach the app's Home screen, at which point the next screen back will be the phone's Home screen.

Don't forget

If your phone is running low on memory it will automatically close any open apps to free up more memory. The ones that have been inactive for the longest period of time are closed first.

Don't forget

New apps for Android phones are available through the Play Store, or directly from the developer's website. They can be downloaded from there and will then appear on your phone. (See pages 130-135.)

Play Store

2 Models of Android Phones

There are a huge number of different Android phones on the market. This chapter looks at some of the leading manufacturers and a few of the phones they make.

RAM stands for Random Access Memory, which is the memory used to process operations that the phone is performing. Usually, the more RAM, the better.

A large number of smartphones, particularly the high-end models, have the capacity for additional storage through the use of a microSD card, which fits into a slot on the side of the body of the phone. This can increase the phone's storage considerably.

Samsung Phones

Samsung is the market leader in terms of the number of smartphones sold globally, partly due to the fact that it offers a considerable range of models, from its flagship Galaxy S models to a range of cheaper models.

Several Samsung smartphones models use the TouchWiz interface as an overlay for Android.

These are some of the Samsung phones to look at.

Galaxy S series

This includes the Galaxy S21 and S21 Ultra, which are Samsung's latest rivals to Apple's iPhone. The specifications include:

- Display: 6.2 inches (diagonally); 6.8 inches for S21 Ultra.

- Weight: 169g; 227g for S21 Ultra.

- RAM: 8GB; 12/16GB for S21 Ultra.

- Memory: 128/256MB; 128/256/512MB for S21 Ultra.

- Operating system: Android 11.

- Main camera: 64MP; 108MP for S21 Ultra.

- Fingerprint sensor for unlocking the phone.

- Battery: Non-removable Li-Ion 4000mAh; 500mAh for S21 Ultra.

Galaxy A series

This is Samsung's mid-range series of phones, and includes the Galaxy A13, Galaxy A03 and Galaxy A52. Some of the specifications for them are (for A13, A03 and A52 respectively):

- Display: 6.5 inches, 6.5 inches, 6.5 inches (diagonally).

- Weight: 195g, 211g, 189g.

- RAM: 4GB, 3/4GB, 6/8GB.

- Memory: Internal – 64GB, 32/64/128GB, 128/256GB.

- Operating system: Android 11.

- Main camera: 50MP, 48MP, 64MP.

- Fingerprint sensor for unlocking the phone, for all.

- Battery: Non-removable Li-Po 5000mAh, 5000mAh, 4500mAh.

Galaxy Z Fold

This is Samsung's folding smartphone, an innovative approach to the development of the smartphone. The specifications include:

- Display: 7.6 inches (diagonally).

- Weight: 271g.

- RAM: 12GB.

- Memory: Internal – 256/512GB.

- Operating system: Android 11.

- Main camera: 12MP.

- Fingerprint sensor for unlocking the phone, side-mounted.

- Battery: Non-removable Li-Po 4400mAh.

Generally, higher-specification models of smartphones – i.e. the most powerful and expensive – come with the latest version of Android, or can upgrade to it. Other models may be limited in terms of the version of Android that they can run.

The phones listed in this chapter are just a small number of the hundreds of Android models that are on the market, covering different specifications and different versions of the Android operating system.

Google Phones

Since Android is owned by Google, it makes sense for them to have their own Android phone. The latest version is the Google Pixel 6 phone, and it comes in the standard model or in the Pro model.

The Pixel 6 is a high-specification smartphone and, unlike the majority of Android phones on the market, comes with the latest version of Android (12 at the time of printing). Also, the Pixel 6 will be the first phone that can update to the next version of Android when it is released.

Android on the Google Pixel 6 is the purest form of the operating system, since – unlike other manufacturers who use Android on their phones – there is no overlay on top of the standard operating system.

The Google Pixel 6

Some of the specifications of the Google Pixel 6 are:

- Display: 6.4 inches (diagonally).

- Weight: 207g.

- RAM: 8GB.

- Memory: Internal – 128/256GB.

- Operating system: Android 12.

- Main camera: 50 MP.

- Fingerprint sensor (below display) for unlocking the phone.

- Battery: Non-removable Li-Ion 4614mAh.

Beware

The Google Pixel 6 does not have a microSD card slot for additional memory, but has unlimited cloud storage for photos.

28

Sony Phones

Sony is another major player in the smartphone market, and has a reputation for producing phones with particularly high-quality cameras.

Xperia 1

The Xperia series is the main range of Sony smartphones, with the Xperia 1 being the flagship model. Some of its specifications are:

- Display: 6.5 inches (diagonally).

- Weight: 186g.

- RAM: 3/4GB.

- Memory: Internal – 256/512GB (upgradable to 1TB using the internal microSD card slot).

- Operating system: Android 11.

- Main camera: 12MP.

- Fingerprint sensor for unlocking the phone, side-mounted.

- Battery: Non-removable Li-Po 4500mAh.

Don't forget

Other Sony smartphones to look at include the Xperia X5 and the Xperia X10.

Motorola Phones

Motorola smartphones are produced by Motorola Mobility, a company that was spun out of the original Motorola. Motorola Mobility was acquired by Google in 2011, and it was then subsequently sold to the Chinese firm Lenovo in 2014. In 2016, Lenovo announced that the Motorola smartphones would use the Moto branding.

Edge S30

The latest flagship Moto smartphone is the Edge S30, and some of its specifications include:

- Display: 6.8 inches (diagonally).

- Weight: 202g.

- RAM: 6-12GB.

- Memory: 128/256GB.

- Operating system: Android 11.

- Main camera: 108MP.

- Fingerprint sensor for unlocking the phone, side-mounted.

- Battery: Non-removable Li-Po 5000mAh.

Other Motorola smartphones to look at include the Moto G200, the Moto G71, and the Moto G51.

HTC Phones

HTC is a Taiwanese company that was at the forefront of the development of smartphones using the Android operating system. Despite an up-and-down performance in the smartphone market, HTC has produced a successful range of phones, with one of the high-end models being the HTC Wildfire E3.

Wildfire E3
The specifications for the HTC Wildfire E3 include:

- Display: 6.52 inches (diagonally).

- Weight: 186g.

- RAM: 3GB.

- Memory: Internal – 64/128GB (upgradable to 1TB using the internal microSD card slot).

- Operating system: Android 10.

- Main camera: 13MP.

- Fingerprint sensor for unlocking the phone, rear-mounted.

- Battery: Non-removable Li-Po 4000mAh.

Other HTC smartphones to look at include the Desire range.

Huawei Phones

Huawei is a major Chinese technology company that produces a wide range of communications devices including smartphones. Most Huawei phones that use Android also use the Emotion User Interface (EMUI) overlay.

nova series

The latest flagship high-end phone from Huawei is the nova 9 (with additional model, the nova 9 Pro), and some of its specifications include:

- Display: 6.57 inches (diagonally).

- Weight: 175g.

- RAM: 8GB.

- Memory: Internal – 128/256GB.

- Operating system: Android with EMUI overlay.

- Main camera: 50MP.

- Fingerprint sensor (below display) for unlocking the phone.

- Battery: Non-removable Li-Po 4300mAh.

Don't forget

Other Huawei smartphones to look at include the P range and the Mate range.

Lenovo Phones

Lenovo is another large Chinese technology company that produces personal computers, laptops, tablets and smartphones, alongside a wide range of other devices.

Lenovo K series
The latest range of Lenovo K series smartphones is the K13. Some of the specifications of the K13 are:

- Display: 6.52 inches (diagonally).

- Weight: 200g.

- RAM: 2GB.

- Memory: Internal – 32GB (upgradable to 1TB using the internal microSD card slot).

- Operating system: Android 10.

- Main camera: 13MP.

- Fingerprint sensor for unlocking the phone, rear-mounted.

- Battery: Non-removable Li-Ion 5000mAh.

Other Lenovo smartphones to look at include the P range.

LG Phones

LG Corporation (formerly Lucky-GoldStar Corporation) is a South Korean multinational that produces a wide range of products, from washing powder and toothpaste to electronic devices. LG Corporation has produced a range of smartphones over the years, with particular success in the US.

W series

The flagship LG smartphone range is the W series, with one of the most recent models being the W41. Some of its specifications include:

- Display: 6.55 inches (diagonally).

- Weight: 201g.

- RAM: 4GB.

- Memory: Internal – 64GB (upgradable to 256GB using the internal microSD card slot).

- Operating system: Android 10.

- Main camera: 48MP.

- Fingerprint sensor for unlocking the phone, rear-mounted.

- Battery: Removable Li-Po 4000mAh.

Other LG smartphones to look at include the K series of budget smartphones.

3 Android Settings

As with all computers and mobile devices, Android phones have a range of settings that can be applied to specify the operation of the device and also its look and feel. This chapter looks at the range of settings that are available, and shows how to apply them to customize your Android phone exactly the way you want it.

Accessing Settings

We all like to think of ourselves as individuals, and this extends to the appearance and operation of our electronic gadgets. An Android phone offers a range of settings so that you can set it up exactly the way you want, and give it your own look and feel. These are available from the **Settings** app.

To access the **Settings** app on your Android phone:

The settings have been updated with Android 10.

1. Swipe up from the bottom of the screen to access the **All Apps** section

2. Tap on the **Settings** app

The Settings app can be added to the Home screen, or the Favorites Tray (see page 56), by pressing and holding on it in the **All Apps** section and then dragging it to the required location.

3. The full range of settings is displayed

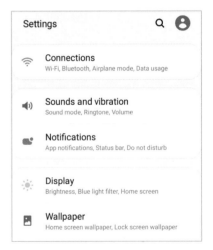

Settings

- **Connections**
  Wi-Fi, Bluetooth, Airplane mode, Data usage
- **Sounds and vibration**
  Sound mode, Ringtone, Volume
- **Notifications**
  App notifications, Status bar, Do not disturb
- **Display**
  Brightness, Blue light filter, Home screen
- **Wallpaper**
  Home screen wallpaper, Lock screen wallpaper

36

The Settings app can also be accessed by swiping down from the top of the phone to access the Quick Settings (see page 54). From here, tap on the **Settings** button at the top of the screen.

4. Tap on an item to view all of the options for it. (If necessary, tap on the options at the next level down to see their own options.) Most options will have an **On/Off** button, a radio button or a checkbox to tap on or off

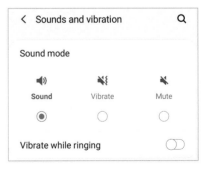

< Sounds and vibration

Sound mode

Sound   Vibrate   Mute

Vibrate while ringing

Connections

These settings can include:

- **Wi-Fi**. Used for turning Wi-Fi on and off on your phone, and connecting to a router.

- **Bluetooth**. Used for connecting wirelessly to other Bluetooth-enabled devices over short distances. Both devices have to be "paired" – i.e. connected together – so that they can share content.

- **NFC and payment**. This can be used to make mobile payments, using a contactless method such as Google Pay, and also connect to other compatible devices, using NFC (Near Field Communication).

- **Airplane mode**. Check this **On** when taking a flight, to disable any mobile communications to or from your phone.

- **Data usage**. Used to view how much data you have downloaded and which apps are using the most data.

- **SIM card manager**. This can be used to apply settings for the SIM card in your phone, and also apply different settings for different SIMs, if your phone supports using more than one.

- **Mobile Hotspot and Tethering**. This can be used to set up your phone as a mobile hotspot so that other devices can connect to it via Wi-Fi, and then connect to the internet.

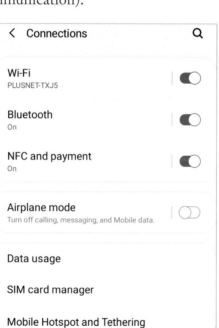

< Connections   Q

Wi-Fi
PLUSNET-TXJ5

Bluetooth
On

NFC and payment
On

Airplane mode
Turn off calling, messaging, and Mobile data.

Data usage

SIM card manager

Mobile Hotspot and Tethering

Hot tip

The **Wi-Fi** setting can be used to connect to Wi-Fi in your own home and also to any public Wi-Fi hotspots. For both, you will usually need to use a password to access the router.

Hot tip

When using settings, tap on the left-facing arrowhead to return to the previous page within a specific setting, or to return to the main Settings Homepage.

< **Connections**

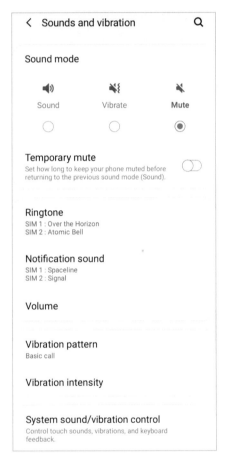

Hot tip

It is worth exploring the sound settings in some detail, as this is where you can turn a lot of the system sounds on and off – e.g. for when notifications and messages are received, keyboard sounds when you are typing, and for the Lock screen. There is also an option for haptic feedback (vibration feedback), which creates a small vibration when pressing certain items.

Sounds and Vibration

These settings can include:

- **Sound mode**. Use this to select from **Sound**, **Vibrate** or **Mute** for the phone's calls and alerts.

- **Temporary mute**. Turn this **On** to mute the phone for a limited period of time after a sound mode.

- **Ringtone**. Use this to select different ringtones to be used on the phone.

- **Notification sound**. Use this to specify sounds for incoming notifications.

- **Volume**. Use this to change the volume for a range of options, including ringtones and notifications.

- **Vibration pattern**. Use this to select the type of vibration, if vibration is turned on.

- **Vibration intensity**. Use this to specify the level of vibration for a range of options.

- **System sound/vibration control**. This includes a range of options for sounds that are used on the phone, including sounds when using the touchscreen and screen lock sounds.

- **Sound quality and effects**. Use this to set sound options, such as using an equalizer to amend the type of sound used on your phone.

Notifications

These settings are used to specify how notifications are dealt with on the phone – i.e. which apps can be activated for showing notifications, and how the notifications are displayed. The options for this are:

- **General notification options**. These apply to all apps and include **Do not disturb**, which can be used to silence all notifications and alerts, regardless of individual app notification settings.

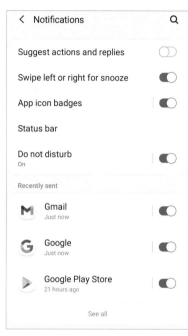

Tap on the **Do not disturb** notification option to apply settings for how this operates, including creating a timed schedule for when Do not disturb is **On**, its duration, and whether notifications are hidden during this time or not.

Tap on the **Show all** option to view a full list of apps. Tap on an app to access individual notifications for the app. For apps that do not have additional options, drag this button **On** to turn on notifications for the app.

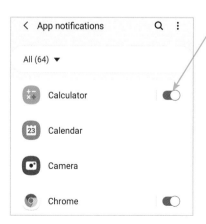

Display

These settings can include:

- **Dark mode settings**. Used to invert the screen colors and use a dark background.

- **Brightness**. Used to set the screen brightness, by dragging the **Brightness** slider.

- **Adaptive brightness**. Used to adjust the screen brightness automatically, based on the current ambient light.

- **Blue light filter**. Used to reduce the amount of blue light that is emitted from the screen.

- **Font size and style**. Used to set the system font size and style for the phone.

- **Screen zoom**. Used to change the size of items on the screen.

- **Full screen apps**. Used to specify which apps can be used in a full-screen aspect ratio, to fill the screen.

- **Screen timeout**. This can be used to specify the length of inactivity before the Lock screen appears.

- **Home screen**. This can be used to change the order of the Home screens on the phone. The screens can be dragged into different positions.

- **Navigation bar**. This can be used for gestures for navigating around the screen, rather than the control buttons on the phone.

- **Screen saver**. Used to display a screen saver when the screen is turned off.

Hot tip

Blue light can make it harder to sleep, so turn **On** the **Blue light filter** setting in the evening. Better still, don't use your phone during the hour before you go to bed.

Hot tip

The **Wallpaper** settings can be used to change the background images for the Home screen and the Lock screen. This can also be done from the Home screen itself – see page 62 for details.

40

Device Care

These settings can include four main categories for keeping your Android phone in good order:

- **Battery**. This displays the health of your phone's battery and has options for optimizing the battery.

- **Storage**. This displays how much of the phone's internal storage capacity has been used and which items are using the storage. It also has an option for freeing up storage space by deleting unnecessary items.

- **Memory**. This shows which apps are currently using the phone's memory and has an option for freeing up more memory by closing apps running in the background.

- **Security**. This has options for scanning your phone for viruses or malware.

Use the **Security** option to frequently scan for viruses or malware that may have infected your phone. See pages 178-179 for information on antivirus apps that can prevent viruses from infecting your phone.

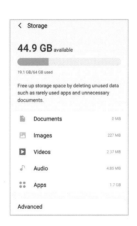

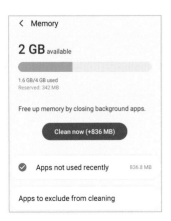

Apps

These settings contain information about apps that are installed on the phone. To view details for apps:

1 Tap on an item on the **All apps** list to view its details

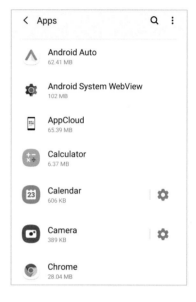

Don't forget

In some cases, the default applications will be linked to the phone's manufacturer – i.e. Samsung phones may use Samsung apps as the default for opening content such as web pages, music and videos.

2 Details about the app are displayed. Tap on the **Disable** button on the bottom toolbar to prevent it from being used, or tap on the **Force stop** button to close it

Biometrics and Security

These settings can include:

- **Face recognition**. For compatible devices, this can be used to set face recognition for unlocking your phone.

- **Fingerprints**. For compatible devices, this can be used to set a unique fingerprint for unlocking your phone.

- **Google Play Protect**. This can be used to automatically scan the apps on your phone for any harmful activity.

- **Security update**. This can be used to view any security updates waiting to be installed for Android.

- **Google Play system update**. This can be used to view any security updates from Google Play.

- **Find My Mobile**. If this is turned **On**, a linked account can be used to find a lost or stolen device, by logging on to the website associated with the account.

- **Install unknown apps**. This can be used to allow apps to be installed from locations other than the Play Store.

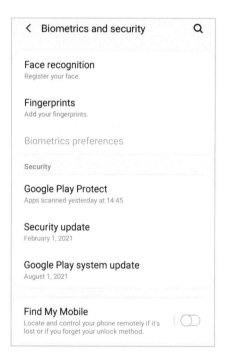

The **Find My Mobile** option will probably be linked to your phone's manufacturer. For a similar option using Google, see **Settings > Google > Find My Device**.

43

- **Encrypt or decrypt SD card**. This can be used to encrypt or decrypt the data on the SD storage card in your phone, if applicable, for security purposes.

- **Other security settings**. This can be a range of security settings, usually specific to your phone's manufacturer.

Accounts and Backup

These settings can include:

- **Accounts, Backup and restore** and a **Cloud** option. The cloud option is related to the phone's manufacturer and will enable you to store items with this online storage and backup service.

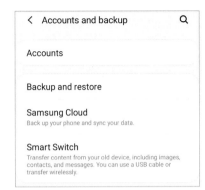

- **Accounts**. This can be used to view existing accounts that are linked to the phone, and add new ones.

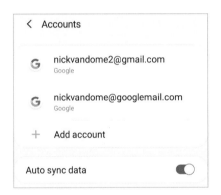

- **Backup and restore**. This can be used to specify how and where items are backed up on the phone and also has options for restoring data from the backup.

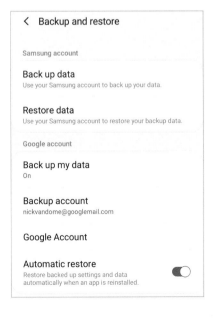

Google

These settings can be used to manage your Google Account. They include:

- **Ads**. This can be used to specify how ads are used on your phone and how they can contact you.

- **Autofill**. This can be used to automatically enter your password into forms on websites.

- **Backup**. This can be used to back up the data on your phone, over Wi-Fi, to the Google storage service. This is a good option for backing up everything on your phone.

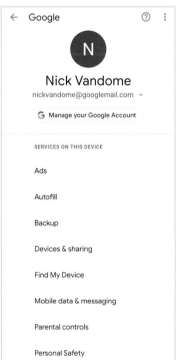

- **Devices & sharing**. This can be used to share the screen of your device, such as to a smart TV, so that you can view items on your phone on a larger screen, which can be useful for items such as watching movies or TV shows.

- **Find My Device**. This can be set up to locate your phone if it is lost or stolen, via the **Find My Device** app (from the Google Play Store) or the **Google Find My Device** web portal.

- **Mobile data & messaging**. This can be used to manage how the data on your phone is used.

- **Parental controls**. This can be used to set restrictions for any children who will be using your phone.

- **Personal Safety**. This can be used to silence notifications when you are driving.

The **Find My Device** option can be used to locate a lost or stolen device, via the Google website, using your Google Account details.

General Management

These settings can include:

For more information about selecting keyboards on an Android phone, see pages 96-97.

- **Language and input**. This can be used to specify the language used by the phone's keyboard, turn the spelling checker on or off, and specify the default virtual keyboard to be used. It can also be used to specify the use of a physical keyboard, connected to the phone.

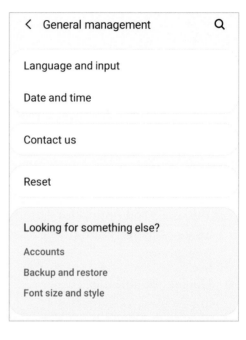

- **Date and time**. This can be used to automatically set the date and the time for the phone, and also specify whether the 24-hour clock format is used or not.

- **Contact us**. This can be used to contact your Android phone's manufacturer, via an online form or website.

Only reset your phone to its original factory settings if you have backed up the content on it – see page 45.

- **Reset**. This can be used to return the phone to its original factory condition and wipe all of the data from it. There are also options to reset specific items, such as the phone's settings.

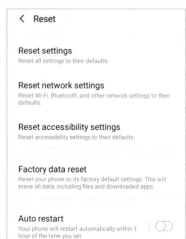

46

Software Update

These settings can include:

- **Download and install**. Tap on this to view if there are any updates waiting to be downloaded. If there is a new update available, details will be displayed. It is possible to schedule a time for the update to be installed, or it can be installed immediately by tapping on the **Install Now** button.

- **Auto download over Wi-Fi**. If this is turned **On**, software updates will be downloaded automatically when they are available, without the need for any manual action. The download will take place when the phone is connected to a Wi-Fi network, to avoid any data charges for downloading.

- **Last update**. This displays information about when the last upload took place.

Keep the software on your Android phone as up-to-date as possible. This will ensure that it runs as efficiently as possible and also contains the latest security updates.

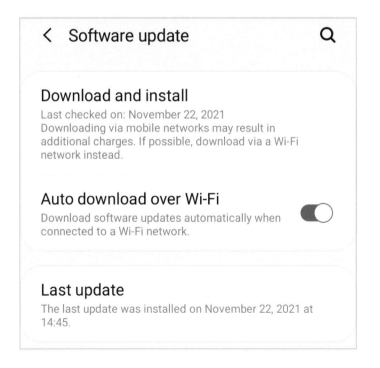

About Phone

These settings can include a range of options, some of them specific to the phone's manufacturer:

- **Phone number**. This contains details of the phone's unique phone number.

- **Model number**. This is the model number of the phone.

- **Serial number**. This is the unique serial number for the phone, and could be useful if the phone is ever stolen.

Beware

If the phone's SIM card is not installed, the phone number will not be displayed under **Phone number**.

< About phone	Q

Galaxy A12

Edit

Phone number	Unknown
Model number	SM-A125F/DSN
Serial number	R58R10VYPLE
IMEI (slot 1)	350396268528336
IMEI (slot 2)	359082628528338

Status
View the SIM card status, IMEI, and other information.

Legal information

Software information
View the currently installed Android version, baseband version, kernel version, build number, and more.

Battery information
View your phone's battery status, remaining power, and other information.

- **Status**. This contains information about items including the phone's SIM card, its address for connecting to networks, and the SIM card's serial number.

- **Legal information**. This contains general legal information about using the phone and the Android operating system.

- **Software information**. This contains details about the current operating system being used by the phone, including the Android version number.

- **Battery information**. This displays information about the current status of the phone's battery, including its charging status and power level.

Advanced Features

These settings can include a range of options, some of them specific to the phone's manufacturer (the examples here are from a Samsung Android phone):

- **Side key**. This can be used to determine the operation of the phone's side key (**On/Off** button).

- **Smart pop-up view**. This can be used to enable notifications to be displayed in their own pop-up window when they are tapped on.

- **Screenshots**. This can be used for options for capturing screenshots, by pressing the **On/Off** button and the **Volume** button.

- **Direct share**. This can be used to share content wirelessly with other people.

- **Reduce animations**. This can be used to reduce the animated effects of items, such as when apps open.

- **Motions and gestures**. This can be used to set various motions to perform certain tasks, such as waking the phone or keeping the screen on when you are viewing it.

- **One-handed mode**. This can be used to display the keyboard at the left-hand or right-hand side of the screen so that it can be used with one hand.

- **Game Launcher**. This contains options for when playing games.

- **Dual Messenger**. This can be used to sign in to various social media apps.

- **Send SOS messages**. If this is turned **On**, you can send an alert to your emergency contacts by pressing the power button three times.

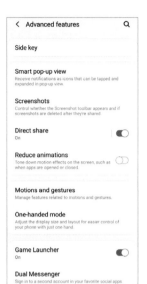

Hot tip

The **Privacy**, **Digital Wellbeing** and **Parental Controls** Settings can be used to protect how your data is used and also have options for improving your overall experience using your Android phone. See pages 180-185 for more details.

Accessibility

It is important for phones to be accessible to as wide a range of users as possible, including those with visual or physical and motor issues. In Android, this is done through the **Accessibility** settings. To use these:

1 Tap on the **Settings** app

2 Tap on the **Accessibility** button

3 The main categories are listed at the top of the window. These are **Visibility enhancements**, **Hearing enhancements**, and **Interaction and dexterity**. Tap on one to view the full range of settings within it

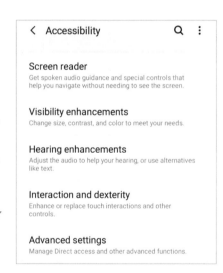

The **Visibility enhancements** section has a **Font size and style** option where the font size can be increased or decreased for compatible apps, display settings and system settings.

Screen reader

1 Tap on the **Screen reader** button in Step 3 above

and tap on the **Voice Assistant** button. Drag the **Voice Assistant** button **On**, whereby the phone will provide spoken information about items on screen and those that are being accessed

To turn off Voice Assistant, tap on the **Voice Assistant** button once in the second Step 1 and then double-tap on it to turn it off.

2 Tap on the **Settings** button at the top of the Voice Assistant window to apply options for how it functions

Experiment with the **Accessibility** settings to become familiar with the functionality of each one.

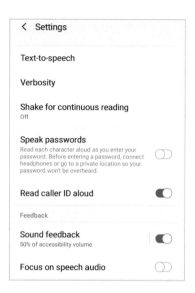

3 Active items are highlighted by a blue outline. Tap once on an item to hear an audio description

4 Tap on **Visibility enhancements** in Step 3 on the previous page to access the setting for zooming on the screen

5 Drag the **Magnifier window** button **On** and press and drag on the magnifier window to increase the magnification of everything within the window

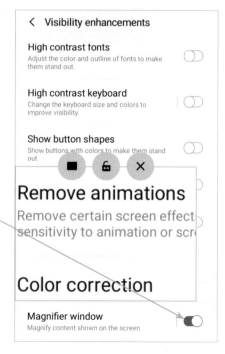

...cont'd

Hearing enhancements
To use some of the **Hearing enhancements** settings:

1 Tap on the **Hearing enhancements** option in Step 3 on page 50

> **Hearing enhancements**
> Adjust the audio to help your hearing, or use alternatives like text.

2 Tap on an option for adapting the device's sound for specific age groups, and tap on the **Personalize your sound** button

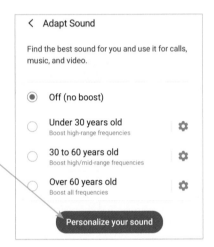

< Adapt Sound

Find the best sound for you and use it for calls, music, and video.

- ⦿ Off (no boost)
- ○ Under 30 years old
  Boost high-range frequencies ⚙
- ○ 30 to 60 years old
  Boost high/mid-range frequencies ⚙
- ○ Over 60 years old
  Boost all frequencies ⚙

Personalize your sound

3 Tap on the **Subtitle settings** option in the **Hearing enhancements** section and drag the **Google subtitles (CC)** button **On** to display subtitles in compatible apps – e.g. for movies or TV shows. Select options for how subtitles are displayed

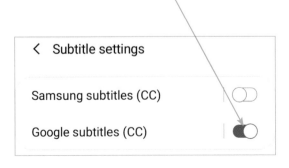

< Subtitle settings

Samsung subtitles (CC)

Google subtitles (CC)

Beware

Only some apps support subtitles, so even if they are turned on they may not appear. Check in an app's specifications in the Play Store (see pages 130-131) to see if it supports subtitles.

52

4 In the **Hearing enhancements** section, below the **Left/right sound balance** heading, drag the slider to the required side to adjust the sound balance when using earphones

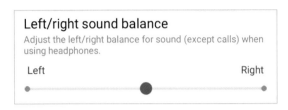

Left/right sound balance
Adjust the left/right balance for sound (except calls) when using headphones.

Left   Right

5 Tap on the **Mono audio** checkbox to use mono if using one earphone

Mono audio
Switch audio from stereo to mono.

Interaction and dexterity settings

To use some of the **Interaction and dexterity** settings:

1 Tap on the **Interaction and dexterity** option in Step 3 on page 50

2 Drag the **Assistant menu** option **On** to create quick access to items

3 Drag the **Interaction control** option **On** to specify areas of the screen that can be inactive to touch

4 Tap on the **Touch and hold delay** option to specify a time period before a key becomes active after pressing and holding it

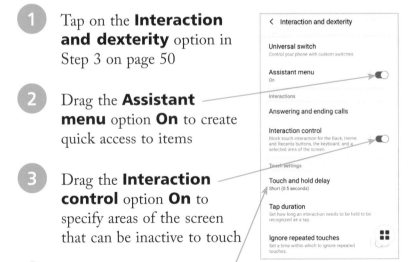

< Interaction and dexterity

Universal switch
Control your phone with custom switches

Assistant menu
On

Interactions

Answering and ending calls

Interaction control
Block touch interaction for the Back, Home, and Recents buttons, the keyboard, and a selected area of the screen.

Touch settings

Touch and hold delay
Short (0.5 seconds)

Tap duration
Set how long an interaction needs to be held to be recognized as a tap.

Ignore repeated touches
Set a time within which to ignore repeated touches.

Beware

Regardless of the sound balance, keep the overall volume on your phone to a reasonable and comfortable level; if it is too loud it may cause long-term damage, particularly when using earphones.

53

Don't forget

If the **Assistant menu** option is turned **On**, this button becomes available. Tap on it to view a range of options, including the **Home** button and the **Volume** button. This icon remains on every screen until the Assistant menu is turned **Off**.

Quick Settings

While the full range of Android settings can be accessed from the **Settings** app, there is also a **Quick Settings** option that can be accessed from the top of the screen. To use this:

Quick Settings has been updated for Android 10.

Tap on the **Menu** button in Step 2 to access options for customizing **Quick Settings**.

Button order
Quick panel layout

1 Swipe down from anywhere at the top of the screen to access **Quick Settings**

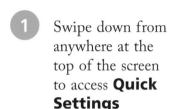

2 Drag down on this button to view the full range of **Quick Settings**

3 Items colored blue are those already in the **Quick Settings** panel. Tap on other items to add them to the panel

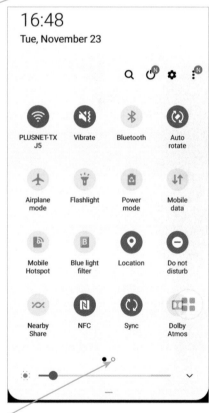

4 Tap on this button to move to other screens of options for adding to the **Quick Settings** panel

4

Around an Android Phone

This chapter details the Android interface and shows how to find your way around the Home screen, add apps and widgets, change the background, and lock your phone. It also covers the sophisticated range of search options that are available, including the digital voice assistant, Google Assistant, and the Hey Google option.

Viewing the Home Screen

Once you have set up your phone, the first screen that you see will be the Home screen. This is also where you will return to when you tap the Home button (see the next page). The elements of the Home screen include:

Hot tip

Swipe down from the Notifications bar to view current notifications, alongside Quick Settings.

Notifications bar   Google Search box

Home screen area. This is where the majority of your commonly used apps and widgets will be located.

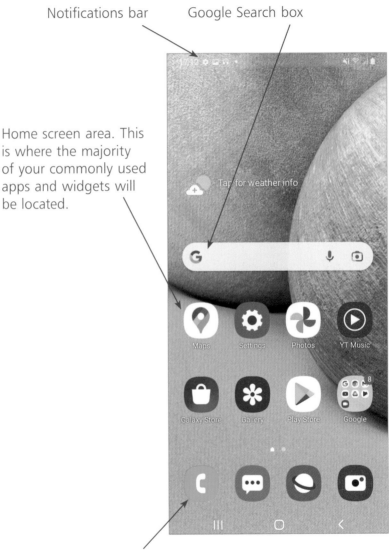

Favorites Tray

Swipe up from the bottom of the Home screen to access the **All Apps** section, which includes all of the apps on the Android phone.

Navigating Around

At the bottom of the Home screen there are three buttons that can be used to navigate around your phone. On some phones these are on the screen, and on others they are on the body of the phone itself.

The navigation buttons are:

Back. Tap on this button to go back to the most recently visited page or screen.

Home. Tap on this button to go back to the most recently viewed Home screen at any point.

Recent Items. Tap on this button to view apps that you have used most recently. Tap on one of the apps to access it again. Swipe an app to the top of the screen to close the app, or tap on the **Close all** button to close all currently open apps.

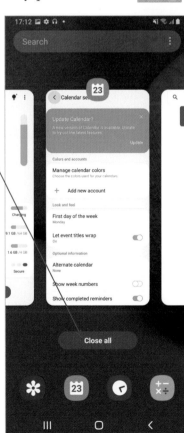

Most Android phones have several Home screens. Swipe left and right to move between them.

When the keyboard is being used, the **Back** button can also be used to hide the keyboard.

If **Swipe gestures** is turned **On** (see page 12) the navigation buttons are not available. This is a new feature in Android 10.

57

Adding Apps

The Home screen is where you can add and manage your apps. To do this:

1 Swipe up from the bottom of the screen to access the **All Apps** section

2 All of the built-in apps are displayed. Tap on an app to open it

3 To add an app to the Home screen, press and hold on it and tap on the **Add to Home** button, or drag it onto the Home screen on which you want it to appear, and release it

4 The app is added to the Home screen

5 Swipe left and right to move between the available Home screens

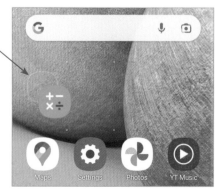

Moving Apps

Once apps have been added to the Home screen they can be repositioned and moved to other Home screens. To do this:

1 Press and hold on an app to move it. A light outline appears, indicating that the app can be repositioned

2 Drag the app and release it to drop it into its new position

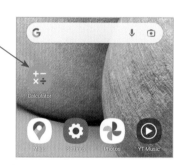

3 To move an app between Home screens, drag it to the edge of the Home screen. As the app reaches the edge of the Home screen it will automatically move to the next one. Add it to the new Home screen in the same way as in Step 2

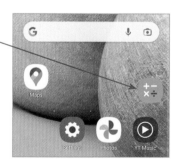

4 Press on an app on the Home screen to view the related options

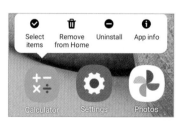

Don't forget

Apps can be moved to the left or right onto new Home screens, if they are available on either side.

Beware

Make sure that the app is fully at the edge of the Home screen, otherwise it will not move to the next one. A thin, light border should appear just before it moves to the next Home screen.

Working with Favorites

The Favorites Tray at the bottom of the Home screen can be used to access the apps you use most frequently. This appears on all Home screens. Apps can be added to or removed from the Favorites Tray, as required.

Don't forget

For some phones, the **Favorites Tray** appears along the bottom of the screen in landscape mode; for others, it appears down the right-hand side of the screen.

Hot tip

Apps can appear in the **Favorites Tray** and also on individual Home screens, but they have to be added there each time from within the **All Apps** section.

1 The apps in the **Favorites Tray** are visible at the bottom of the screen on all Home screens

2 Press and hold on an app in the **Favorites Tray** and drag it onto the Home screen to remove it from the Favorites Tray

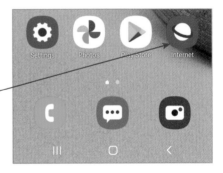

3 Press and hold on an app on the Home screen, and drag it onto a space in the **Favorites Tray** to add it there

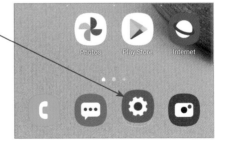

4 The **Favorites Tray** has a limit to the number of apps that it can contain, and if you try to add more than this, the app will spring back to its original location

Adding Widgets

Android widgets are similar to apps, except that they generally display specific content or real-time information. For instance, a photo gallery widget can be used to display photos directly on a Home screen, or a traffic widget can display updated information about traveling conditions. Widgets can be added from any Home screen.

Hot tip

From the panel in Step 1 you can also access wallpapers (see page 62).

1 Press and hold on an empty area on any Home screen and tap on the **Widgets** button

Wallpaper   Themes   Widgets   Home screen settings

2 Swipe up and down, or sometimes left and right, to view all available widgets

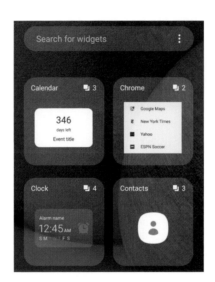

Search for widgets

Calendar   3

346
days left
Event title

Chrome   2

Google Maps
New York Times
Yahoo
ESPN Soccer

Clock   4

Alarm name
12:45 AM
S M T F S

Contacts   3

Don't forget

Widget icons on Home screens usually appear larger than those for standard apps.

3 Press and hold on a widget and drop it onto a Home screen as required, in the same way as for adding apps

Maps   Galaxy Store

WED, ...   +

Tue, November 30

St Andrew'...
All day

Calculator   Gallery

Changing the Background

The background (wallpaper) for all of the Home screens on your phone can be changed within the **Settings** app (**Settings** > **Wallpaper**). However, it can also be changed directly from any Home screen. To do this:

1 Press and hold on an empty area on any Home screen and tap on the **Wallpaper** button

Wallpaper

2 Tap on the **My wallpapers** option

3 Tap on one of the wallpaper options

Hot tip

Wallpaper apps can be downloaded from the Play Store, to add a wider range of backgrounds to your phone. Enter "**wallpaper**" into the Search box of the **Apps** section of the Play Store.

62

4 Select whether the background is for the **Home screen**, the **Lock screen**, or both

Set as wallpaper

Home screen

Lock screen

Lock and Home screens

5 For the option selected in Step 4, tap on the **Set on [Home] screen** button

Set on Home screen

Creating Folders

As you start to use your Android phone for more activities, you will probably acquire more and more apps. These will generally be for a range of tasks covering areas such as productivity, communications, music, photos, and so on. Initially it may be easy to manage and access these apps, but as the number of them increases, it may become harder to keep track of them all.

One way in which you can manage your apps is to create folders for apps covering similar subjects – e.g. one for productivity apps, one for entertainment apps; etc. To create folders for different apps:

1 Drag one app over another

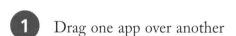

2 A folder is created, and the app is added to the folder. Tap here to give the folder a name

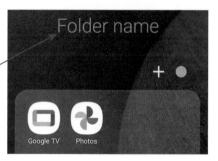

3 Enter the name, and tap on the **+** button to add more items to the folder

4 Tap on the required items to select them for adding to the folder

Don't forget

To remove an app from a folder, press and hold on it and drag it out of the folder onto a Home screen.

Hot tip

Adding folders to the Favorites Tray is a good way to make a larger number of apps available here.

63

Using Notifications

Android phones have numerous ways of keeping you informed, from new emails and calendar events to the latest information about apps that have been downloaded and installed. To make it easier to view these items, they are grouped together in the Notification panel. This appears on the Lock screen and can also be accessed from any Home screen by swiping down from the Notifications bar.

1 By default, some notifications are shown on the Lock screen. Tap on a notification here to access it directly (you must unlock your phone first – see pages 66-67)

2 On any Home screen or the **All Apps** screen, notifications are indicated on the Notifications bar

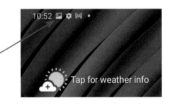

Tap on the **Clear** button at the bottom of the Notification panel to clear all current notifications. If you clear notifications it does not delete items; they remain within their relevant apps and can be viewed there.

3 Swipe down from the top of any screen to access your notifications. Some of these may display more details than on the Lock screen

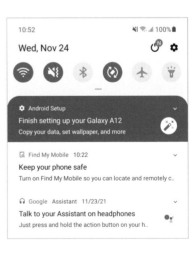

4 Tap on a notification to view its full details within the relevant app – e.g. a Gmail notification will open Gmail to view new emails

Screen Rotation

By default, the content on a phone's screen rotates as you rotate the device. This means that the content can be viewed in portrait or landscape mode, depending on what is being used – e.g. for websites it may be preferable to have it in landscape mode, while for reading it may be better in portrait mode:

Don't forget

Screen rotation is achieved by a gyroscope sensor in the phone.

It is also possible to lock the screen so that it does not rotate when you move it. This can be useful if you are using it for a specific task and do not want to be distracted by the screen rotating if you move your hand slightly. To lock and unlock the screen rotation:

Hot tip

The **Auto rotate** button is sometimes called **Screen rotation** on other Android models.

1 Drag down from the top of the screen to access **Quick Settings**

2 Tap on the **Auto rotate** button to enable screen rotation

3 Tap on the **Auto rotate** button again to lock the screen so that the screen will not rotate with the phone

Locking Your Phone

Security is an important issue for any computing device, and this applies to physical security as much as online security. For Android phones, it is possible to place a digital lock on the screen so that only someone who knows the details of the lock can open it. There are different ways in which a lock can be set.

1 Tap on the **Settings** app

2 Tap on the **Lock screen** button

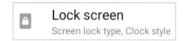
	Lock screen
	Screen lock type, Clock style

3 The current method of **Screen lock type** is displayed here. Tap on this to access the options

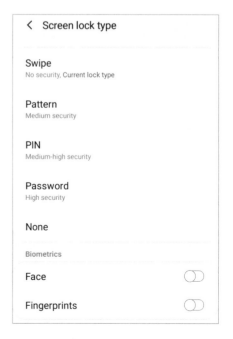

4 The methods for locking the screen are **Swipe**, **Pattern**, **PIN**, **Password**, **None**, **Face** (if applicable) and **Fingerprints** (if applicable). Tap on the required method to select it and set its attributes

Beware

The **Swipe** option is the least secure and is only really useful for avoiding items being activated accidentally when your phone is not in use; it is not a valid security method. The most secure method is a password containing letters, numbers and symbols, or fingerprints.

5 For the **PIN** (or **Password**) option, enter your chosen PIN in the box and tap on the **Continue** button. Enter the PIN again for confirmation. This will then need to be entered whenever you want to unlock the phone

PIN stands for Personal Identification Number, and is a sequence of numbers chosen by and known only to you.

6 For the **Pattern** option, drag over the keypad to create the desired pattern, repeat to confirm, and this will then be enabled on your Lock screen

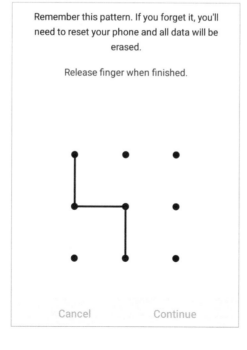

Whenever your phone goes to sleep it will need to be unlocked before you can use it again. Sleep mode can be activated by pressing the **On/Off** button once. After a period of inactivity it will go into Sleep mode automatically: the length of time until this happens can be specified within **Settings > Display > Screen timeout**.

67

Searching

Since Android is owned by Google, it is unsurprising that phones with this operating system come with the power of Google's search functionality. Items can be searched for within the phone itself, or you can perform searches on the web. This can be done by typing in the Google Search box and also by using the voice search option. To search for items on an Android phone:

1 The Google Search box is usually found on the Home screen, or it can be accessed through the

Google app or added via a widget (see page 61)

2 Begin typing a word or phrase. As you type, corresponding suggestions will appear, both for on the web and for apps on the phone (if applicable)

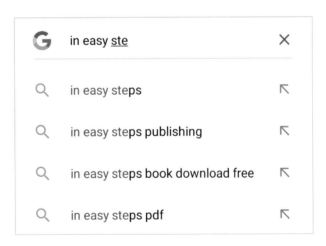

3 As you continue to type, the suggestions will become more defined

Don't forget

On some phones, the search option is indicated by a magnifying glass with the word "Google" next to it.

4 Tap on an app result to open it directly on your phone, or tap on this button on the keyboard to view results from the web

Voice search

To use the voice search functionality on your phone, instead of typing a search query:

Hot tip

The voice search functionality can also be used for items such as finding directions, setting alarms and finding photos on your phone.

1 Tap on the microphone button in the Search box

2 When the colored dots appear, speak the word or phrase for which you want to search

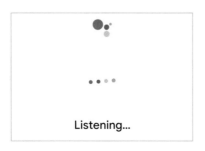

Listening...

...cont'd

3 You can use voice search to find or open items on your phone or from the web. On your phone you can use voice search to open apps, such as your Gmail app

open the Play Store

4 The app opens in the same way as if you had tapped on it from the Home screen

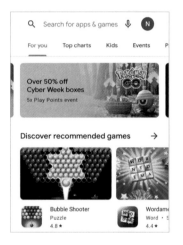

Don't forget

The phrase displayed in the voice search window is sometimes a summary of what you actually say. For instance, if you say, **"Please open Gmail app"**, the words **"open gmail"** may be displayed.

5 If you search for items on the web, Google will use your location (if enabled) and also your search history to give you more accurate results. For instance, if you search for **"Indian restaurants"** it will display the results for those closest to your location

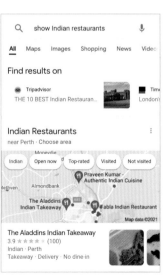

Google Assistant Search

One innovation from Google on some Android phones is Google Assistant. This is a personal digital assistant that responds to voice commands. To use Google Assistant:

1 Press and hold on the **Home** button to start setting up Google Assistant

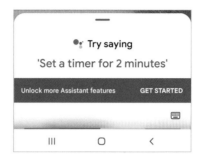

Once Google Assistant has been set up it is always available.

2 Tap on the **Get Started** button to set up Google Assistant, to offer suggestions based on what is on your screen and also what you have searched for previously

GET STARTED

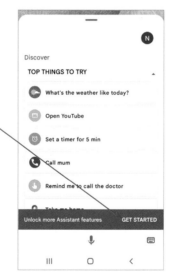

After you have set up Google Assistant, press and hold on the **Home** button to access it from any Home screen or app.

3 Queries can be made of Google Assistant, using voice or text options

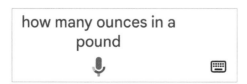

...cont'd

4 Speak the query, such as "find the nearest coffee shop"

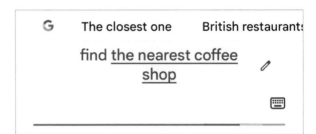

Hot tip

Google Assistant is an excellent option for finding locations when you are traveling. However, this requires a Wi-Fi or cellular network connection, with 3G, 4G or 5G.

Don't forget

Location must be checked **On** (**Settings** > **Location**) for these services to work.

6 Google Assistant displays the results. There are also options for searching for results over the web and viewing them on a map, if applicable

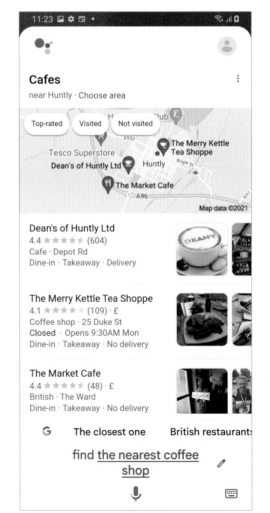

Hey Google

Google Assistant also incorporates the "Hey Google" functionality, whereby you can use voice search commands from any screen. To set up Hey Google:

1 Tap on the **Google** app

2 Tap on the **Account** button

3 Tap on the **Settings** option

4 Tap on the **Google Assistant** option

5 Tap on the **Hey Google & Voice Match** option

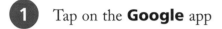
✓ Hey Google & Voice Match
Get hands-free help from your Assistant

6 Drag the **Hey Google** button **On** to enable the Assistant to be enabled when you say, "Hey Google" from any screen on your phone

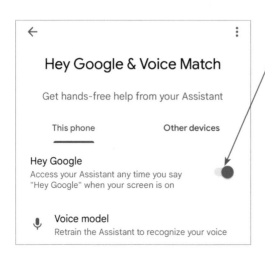

← ⋮

Hey Google & Voice Match

Get hands-free help from your Assistant

This phone   Other devices

Hey Google
Access your Assistant any time you say
"Hey Google" when your screen is on

🎤 Voice model
Retrain the Assistant to recognize your voice

Beware

It may take Hey Google longer to recognize regional accents, but it should identify them after a bit of practice.

Hot tip

Tap on the **Voice model** option in Step 6 to train Google to recognize your own voice more easily.

Using Google Discover

We live in an age where we want the availability of as much up-to-date information as possible. On an Android phone, one option for this is Google Discover, accessed from the Google app. This is a digital assistant service that can be customized to provide exactly the information you want.

Accessing Google Discover

Google Discover works closely with the Google Assistant and can display a similar range of information. It can be accessed from the Google app.

Google Discover has been updated in Android 10.

1 Tap on the **Google** app

2 Tap on the **Discover** button at the bottom of the screen to view the latest news items from Google Discover

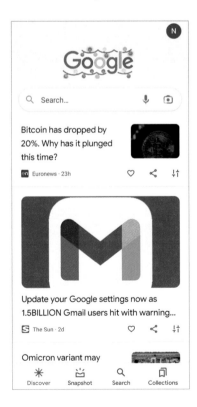

3 Tap on the **Snapshot** button at the bottom of the screen

Snapshot

4 The **Snapshot** section can include news items for topics you have selected, reminders you have set, shopping list items and notes you have made

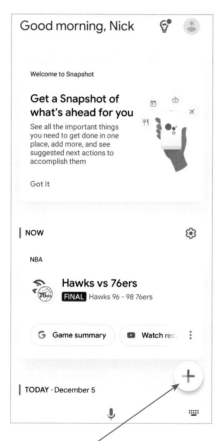

To use Google Discover on your phone, you have to be connected to the internet via Wi-Fi or cellular.

5 Tap on the **Add** button to add new categories to the **Snapshot** section, including reminders, shopping items and notes

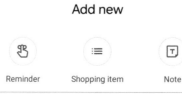

...cont'd

6 Tap on the **Collections** button at the bottom of the screen

Collections

7 The **Collections** section can be used to create folders and pin items that you have searched for into folders. This can be a good way to collate similar subject matter from the web so that it is all available in the same place. Tap on the **New** button in the top right-hand corner to create a new collection

+ **New**

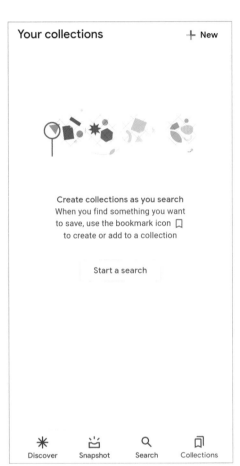

Your collections   + New

Create collections as you search
When you find something you want
to save, use the bookmark icon 🔖
to create or add to a collection

Start a search

✳ Discover   ☐ Snapshot   🔍 Search   🔖 Collections

Hot tip

Give each collection a quickly identifiable name so that you can locate the required collection, even when there are a significant number of them.

8 Enter a name for the new collection and tap on the **Create** button

✕ New collection   Create

Family

9 Tap on the **Search for things to add** button

10 Enter a topic into the Google Search box and tap on one of the results

11 Navigate to a page to add it to a collection and tap on the bookmark icon

12 The selected item is added to the collection and it can be opened from here at any time. Add similar content to build up a collection of similar items

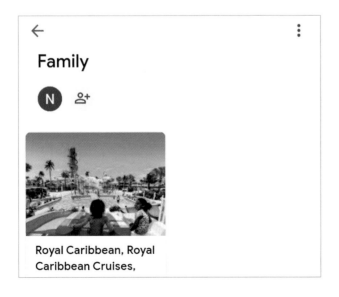

Collections are not the same as bookmarks that are created in a web browser, such as Chrome. Bookmarks on the web are favorite pages that are selected and stored in the **Bookmarks** folder within the browser.

...cont'd

13 Tap on the account icon at the top of the Google Discover window to access options for managing your Google Account

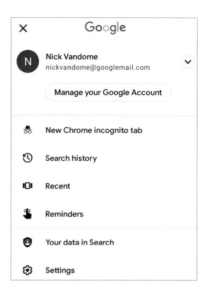

14 Tap on the **Settings** option to access settings for your Google Account and also Google Assistant

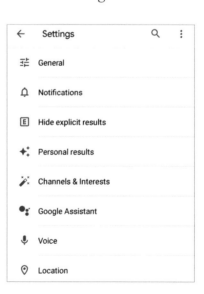

5 Calls and Contacts

This chapter focuses on using an Android phone to make and receive calls, and also how to add details of people who have contacted you.

Adding Contacts

Given the range of uses to which you can put your Android phone, it is sometimes overlooked that one of its original functions is to make phone calls to people. This can be done by typing a number directly into the phone dialer (see page 88). However, it is generally better to first add contacts to your phone, and then you can use these details to keep in touch with them in a variety of ways. To add a contact:

The Contacts option can also be accessed from the **Phone** app, from the Contacts tab.

1 Tap on the **Contacts** app

2 By default, the **Contacts** app will only show details of the SIM card currently installed. Tap on the **+** button to add a new contact to your Contacts list

3 Select where you want to store the contact. Generally, it is better to store contacts on the SIM card, rather than the phone, so that if you get a new phone you can move all of your contacts by simply transferring the SIM card. It can also be stored to Google, which stores it online, and this can be accessed through your Google Account

If you have a Google Account, contacts can be added here too, in Step 3, so that they are available from the **Contacts** app and the **Phone** app.

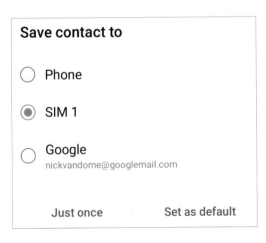

80

4 Enter details for the new contact and tap on the **Save** button at the bottom of the screen

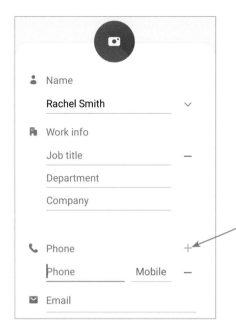

Hot tip

Tap on the **+** button next to a category to add more options for it – e.g. to add a home phone number and a mobile one too.

5 The new contact is added to the **Contacts** app (which is also accessed from the **Contacts** tab in the **Phone** app)

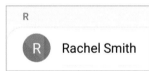

6 Tap on a contact to see their details. Tap on the speech bubble icon to create a text message for the selected contact, the phone icon to make a call to them, or the video icon to make a video call

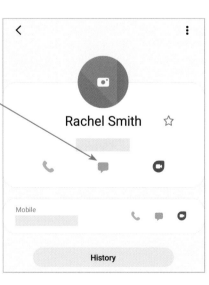

Saving Contacts from Calls

Another quick way to add a contact is to ask someone to phone you so that you can then copy their number directly from your phone to your contacts. You do not even have to answer the phone to do this.

Don't forget

When you receive a call while you are using another app, accept it by tapping the green **Answer** button. To reject a call, tap the red **Decline** button.

1 Once someone has phoned, tap on the **Phone** button

2 Tap on the **Recents** tab. The call or text will be displayed

3 Tap on the **+ Add to Contacts** option

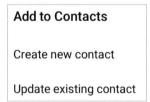

4 Select whether to **Create new contact** or **Update existing contact**

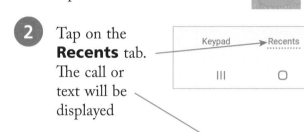

Don't forget

The **Recents** page shows the most recent calls and texts you have received.

5 Enter details for the contact and add them to the **Contacts** app in the same way as on page 81

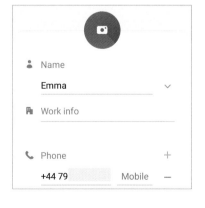

Saving Contacts from Texts

Contacts can also be saved from text messages.

1 Open the **Messages** app. Tap on the **Conversations** tab and tap on a conversation

2 Tap on the **Add to contacts** button

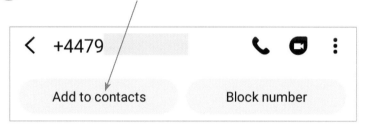

3 Select how to add the contact and add them to the **Contacts** app in the same way as on page 81

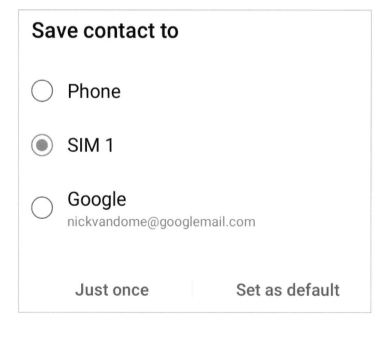

Someone can send you a blank text just so that you can add their details to your contacts.

If someone is already in your contacts but you do not have their cell/mobile number included, or you want to update an existing number, tap on **Update existing** after tapping on **Add to contacts** in Step 2 to add the number to their existing details.

Managing Contacts

Sometimes you may end up with contacts on your phone (if you have selected to save them onto your device rather than the SIM card) and you will want to transfer them to your SIM card. This is useful if you are going to transfer your SIM card to another phone. To do this:

1 Tap on the **Contacts** app

2 Tap on the **Menu** button at the top left-hand side of the window

3 Tap on the **Manage contacts** option

⚙

👤 All contacts   252

Groups   ⌄

Manage contacts

Trash

4 Tap on the **Import or export contacts** option

‹ Manage contacts

≫ **Merge contacts**
Merge contacts with the same name, phone number, or email address.

Import or export contacts
Import contacts to your phone or export them to another location.

☁ **Move contacts**
Move contacts between your phone and accounts.

↻ **Sync contacts**

◑ **Default storage location**

Beware

If there is no SIM card available, the **Import or export contacts** option will only be available with your device's internal storage.

5 Tap on the **Import** or **Export** button to start the transfer of contacts

6 Options for exporting (or importing, if this is selected in Step 5) are displayed, usually to internal storage on the phone, or to the phone's SIM card

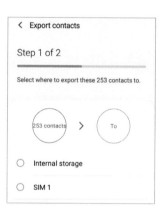

7 Tap on the required option – e.g. **Internal storage** – and tap on the **Export** button to export (or **Import**, if this is selected in Step 5) your contacts

Once contacts have been exported, they can be shared to other people, using the .vcf file format in Step 8.

8 Once the operation has been completed, this is shown within the Notification panel

⬆ Contacts

Contacts.vcf exported.

Editing Contacts

Once contacts have been added to your Android phone you can still edit their details, whether they have been added to the phone or the SIM card, although a wider range of information can be added to a contact on the phone.

1 Tap on the **Contacts** app

2 Access a contact and tap on their name to view their details

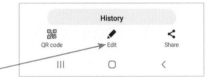

3 The current details are displayed. Tap on the **Edit** button on the bottom toolbar

4 Edit the details as required. Contacts that have been added to the phone's storage have a greater range of fields for information. If the contact has only been added to the SIM card, the only fields available will be for name and phone number

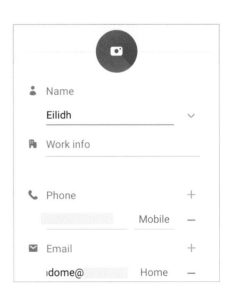

Hot tip

If you have downloaded messaging apps such as WhatsApp, the information from your Contacts list will be synced with this, and any of your contacts who are using the service will automatically be displayed in the messaging app, if you agree to this when you install the WhatsApp app.

5 Tap on an item to view its options

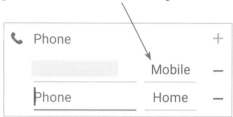

6 Select options as required

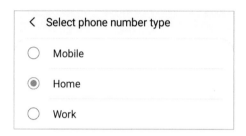

7 Tap on the **Save** button to save the editing changes

Save

8 Tap on the green **+** button next to an item to add an additional field for it – i.e. if you want to add more than one phone number for a contact

Beware

If a contact has more than one phone number, make sure that you select the required one when phoning or text messaging them.

Making a Call

Once you have added contacts to your phone, there are a number of ways in which you can phone them.

Typing a number

You can make a call by accessing the phone dialer and typing a contact's number on the keypad. To do this:

You can also create shortcuts to speed dial specific contacts, by pressing and holding a digit on the keypad and tapping **Assign**, then selecting a contact from your Contacts list. Once set up, you can then just press and hold that digit to dial that particular number.

1   Tap on the **Phone** app

2   Tap on the **Keypad** button at the bottom of the screen. Type the person's number on the keypad. As the number is entered, corresponding names will be displayed from your Contacts list

Keypad

Tap on this button in Step 4 to make a video call to someone with a compatible device (i.e. another Android phone that supports video calls), instead of a voice call:

3   Tap on the contact's name to display their full number

4   Tap on the **Call** button to call the number

Searching for a contact

Once you have added contacts to your Contacts list, you can access them and then call them. To do this:

1 Tap on the **Phone** app

2 Tap on the **Contacts** tab. At the top of the Contacts list is a Search box

3 Tap in the Search box and type a name you want to find

4 All matching results are shown. The more characters of a name that you type, the more the search results will be narrowed down.

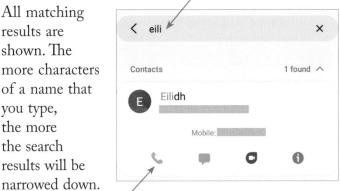

Tap on the phone icon to call the contact

Making a quick call

It is also possible to place a call to a contact in your Contacts list, just using one swipe. To do this:

1 Access the Contacts list

2 Swipe to the right on the contact's name. A green **Call** button appears and the call is connected automatically

Hot tip

Swipe to the left on a contact's name to send them a text message, rather than make a call.

Receiving a Call

When you receive a call, the caller's name will show up on the screen (if they are in your contacts), accompanied by a ringtone (see pages 93-94).

Hot tip

On some Android models, if the caller has sent you any text messages, the latest one will be displayed on the **Incoming call** screen.

Hot tip

Tap on the **Send message** button in Step 2 to reject the call but send the caller a text message instead.

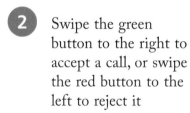

1 When a call is received, the caller's name is displayed (if they have been added as a contact) along with their phone number. If their photo has been added to their contact details, this will be displayed too

2 Swipe the green button to the right to accept a call, or swipe the red button to the left to reject it

3 If you are using another app when a call is received, the full-size window is minimized to a smaller one. Tap on **Answer** or **Decline**

4 Once a call has been accepted, these buttons appear at the bottom of the window, when in full screen

Tap on the **Bluetooth** button in Step 4 to connect your phone to a Bluetooth headset or headphones so that you can take the call hands-free.

5 Tap on the **Keypad** button to access a keypad that can be used during the call – i.e. if you are selecting options during an automated call

6 Tap on the **Speaker** button to activate the speaker so that you can hear the call without holding the phone to your ear

7 The Home screen, or other apps, can be accessed during a call by pressing

the **Home** button, in which case the call window is minimized at the top of the screen

...cont'd

8 During a call in full screen, tap on the **Menu** button at the top of the call window

9 Select options for the call, including **View contact** and **Send message**

View contact

Send message

10 Tap on the **End call** button to end the current call

11 Once a call has been ended, tap on these buttons to **View contact** or call them back with a **Call**, **Message** or **Video call (Duo)**

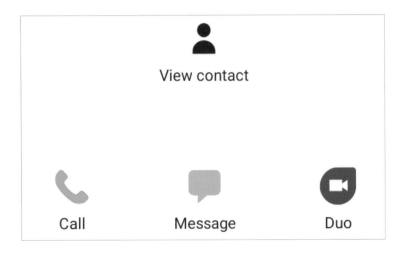

View contact

Call   Message   Duo

Don't forget

The Duo app is Google's video-chatting app.

Setting Ringtones

Ringtones were one of the original must-have accessories that helped transform the way people looked at mobile/cell phones. Android phones have a range of ringtones that can be used, and you can also download and install thousands more. To use the default ringtones:

1 Tap on the **Settings** app

2 Tap on the **Sounds and vibration** button

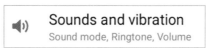

🔊 **Sounds and vibration**
Sound mode, Ringtone, Volume

3 Tap on one of the **Ringtone** options for ringtones for when you receive a phone call

Ringtone
→ SIM 1 : Over the Horizon
SIM 2 : Atomic Bell

4 Tap on one of the options to hear a preview. With the desired tone selected, tap on the **+** button to select the ringtone for your phone

‹ Ringtone	**+**
○ Haze	
○ Homecoming	
○ Icecubes	
○ Interstellar	
⦿ Over the Horizon	
○ Pick It Up	
○ Pulse	

Beware

Do not give too many unique ringtones to different people, otherwise it may be difficult to remember them all when people phone.

...cont'd

Getting more ringtones

While the default ringtones will serve a perfectly good purpose, there is also a wealth of sounds and music that can be downloaded and used as ringtones. This can be done through the Google Play Store.

Beware

Experimenting with different ringtones can be good fun, but after a while you may find that they can become slightly irritating for you and those nearby.

1 Access the Google Play Store app. Tap on the Search box and enter **ringtones** to see the available options

2 Tap on one of the search results

3 Tap on one of the ringtone apps to download it

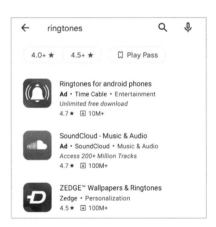

4 Open the app and download one of the ringtones in the app. This will then be available in the list in Step 4 on page 93. Select it and tap on the **+** button to use it as a ringtone

6 Using the Keyboard

This chapter looks at entering text and data with the keyboard on an Android phone, focusing on the widely available Google keyboard: Gboard.

Keyboards with Android

All Android phones have a keyboard, for inputting text and data, and the vast majority of them are virtual ones – i.e. they appear on the screen, rather than an actual physical keyboard. Different phone manufacturers add their own keyboards to their specific handsets, and this is usually the default keyboard that appears. However, different keyboards can be downloaded from the Play Store, including the Google keyboard (Gboard), which is a good, multi-purpose Android keyboard. To download different keyboards:

Don't forget

As the Google keyboard is produced by Google, it can be considered the default Android keyboard and is used for the examples in this chapter.

1 Access the Play Store and type **android keyboard** into the Search box

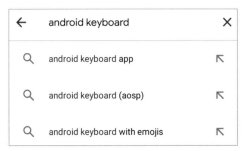

←	android keyboard	✕
Q	android keyboard app	↖
Q	android keyboard (aosp)	↖
Q	android keyboard with emojis	↖

2 Tap on one of the search results to view the keyboard app and download and install it, if required

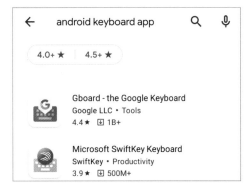

← android keyboard app   Q   🎤

4.0+ ★   4.5+ ★

Gboard - the Google Keyboard
Google LLC • Tools
4.4★   ⊡ 1B+

Microsoft SwiftKey Keyboard
SwiftKey • Productivity
3.9★   ⊡ 500M+

3 The keyboard app will be added to the next available Home screen. Tap on it to set it up and also access its settings once setup is completed

Microsoft SwiftKey Key...

Selecting Keyboards

Several different keyboards can be installed and used on your Android phone. Keyboards can be changed at any time and different ones selected. To do this:

1 Tap on **Settings** and select **General Management**

2 Tap on the **Language and input** option

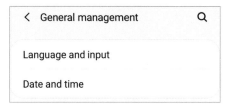

3 Tap on the **On-screen keyboard** option

4 The available keyboards are listed. Tap on one to view its details and select it as the default

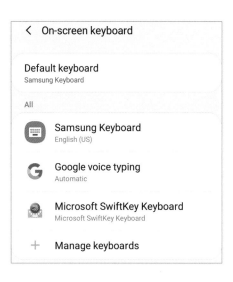

Most Android phone manufacturers include their own keyboards on their phones and these are the default ones that are used, until a different one is selected.

About the Google Keyboard

As with other Android keyboards, the Google keyboard (Gboard) can be used for a variety of actions:

- Entering text with a messaging app, word processing app, email app or a notes app.

- Entering a web address.

- Entering information into a form.

- Entering a password.

Viewing the keyboard

When you attempt one of the tasks above, the keyboard appears before you can enter any text or numbers:

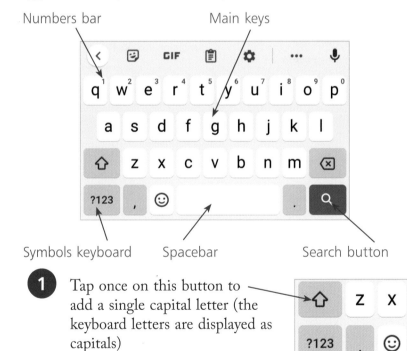

Numbers bar · Main keys

Symbols keyboard · Spacebar · Search button

Don't forget

When using the keyboard for normal text or data entry, it only requires a light touch: you do not have to press very hard on the keys.

Don't forget

The Numbers bar on the Gboard is permanently available as part of the top row of letters: press and hold on a letter to add the number above it.

Don't forget

Caps Lock means that all letters will be entered as capital letters.

1 Tap once on this button to add a single capital letter (the keyboard letters are displayed as capitals)

2 Tap on this button again to create **Caps Lock** (if caps are activated as in Step 1; double-tap if not). This is indicated by the solid line below the arrow

...cont'd

3 Tap once on this button to back-delete an item

4 Tap once on this button to access the **Symbols** keyboard option

5 Tap on this button to access the second page of the **Symbols** keyboard

6 Tap once on this button on either of the **Symbols** keyboards above to return to the standard **QWERTY** option

Tap on this button to access the number pad for entering numerical data:

Sometimes, the button in Step 5 is **1/2** or **2/2**. Tap these buttons to move between the **Symbols** pages.

If you are entering a password, or details into a form, the keyboard will have a **Go** or **Send** button that can be used to activate the information that has been entered.

Keyboard Settings

There are a number of options for setting up the functionality of the Google keyboard. These can be accessed in two ways:

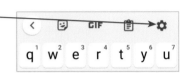
Gboard

1 Tap on the **Gboard** app; or

2 Tap on the **Settings** button on the top shortcuts bar of the Google keyboard

3 A full list of keyboard settings is displayed

4 Tap on the **Languages** option to select different languages

5 Tap on the **Theme** option to select a colored theme for the keyboard

6 Tap on the **Dictionary** option for creating a personal dictionary that lets you add your own words to the dictionary, and also shortcuts for frequently used words or names

← Settings   ⋮

🌐 Languages
English (US) (QWERTY)

⊟ Preferences

◉ Theme

A⌄ Text correction

〽 Glide typing

🎤 Voice typing

📋 Clipboard

📖 Dictionary

☺ Emojis, Stickers & GIFs

⦉ Share Gboard

⋯ Advanced

★ Rate us

Don't forget

Tap on the **Preferences** button in Step 3 to access a range of options for the keys on the keyboard, and layout and key press options such as for sounds and vibrations for when keys are pressed.

Don't forget

Most keyboards have a setting for **Predictive text**. This is a function where words are suggested as you type them: as more letters are added to the word, the suggestion becomes more defined. In the Gboard app, this functionality is provided by the **Show suggestion strip** option (see the next page).

100

7 Tap on the **Text correction** button on the previous page, to access options for working with text as it is being written

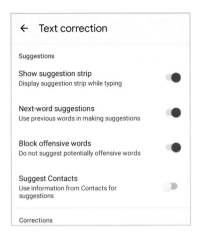

← Text correction

Suggestions

Show suggestion strip
Display suggestion strip while typing

Next-word suggestions
Use previous words in making suggestions

Block offensive words
Do not suggest potentially offensive words

Suggest Contacts
Use information from Contacts for suggestions

Corrections

The **Show suggestion strip** option in Step 7 displays suggested words as you type (tap on one to select it); **Next-word suggestions** displays a possible next word, based on the one just used; and **Suggest Contacts** displays names from the Contacts app.

8 Drag **On** or **Off** the buttons for **Show suggestion strip**, **Next-word suggestions**, **Block offensive words** and **Suggest Contacts**

9 Scroll down the **Text correction** page to access options for **Auto-correction**, **Undo auto-correct on backspace**, **Auto-capitalization**, **Double-space period** and **Spelling** options. Drag the buttons **On** or **Off** as required to apply or disable the settings

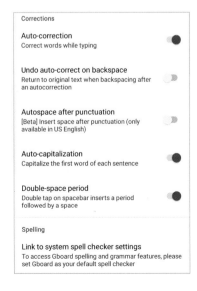

Corrections

Auto-correction
Correct words while typing

Undo auto-correct on backspace
Return to original text when backspacing after an autocorrection

Autospace after punctuation
[Beta] Insert space after punctuation (only available in US English)

Auto-capitalization
Capitalize the first word of each sentence

Double-space period
Double tap on spacebar inserts a period followed by a space

Spelling

Link to system spell checker settings
To access Gboard spelling and grammar features, please set Gboard as your default spell checker

The **Auto-correction** option lets you insert the currently highlighted word by tapping on the spacebar; **Auto-capitalization** automatically inserts a capital letter at the start of a new sentence; **Double-space period** adds a period/full stop when the spacebar is tapped twice.

Gboard Suggestion Strip

At the top of the Gboard keyboard (and most other Android keyboards) is the Suggestion strip, if suggestions are turned on (see page 101). To use the Suggestion strip:

1 Tap on this button to hide the Suggestion strip

2 Tap on this button to display the Suggestion strip

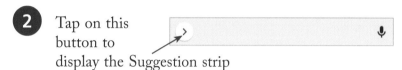

3 Tap on this button to access **Stickers** to add to a message

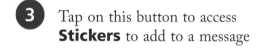

4 Tap on this button to select animated **GIF** images to add to a message

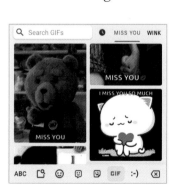

Voice typing can also be accessed from the Suggestion strip by tapping on this button:

5 Tap on this button to access the **Clipboard**, where items have been copied to the clipboard so that they can be pasted into a message. Tap on the **Turn on Clipboard** button if this is not already **On**

 Copy more for faster pasting

Gboard's clipboard lets you copy text and images, keeping them for 1 hour, to quickly paste many things at once.

Turn on Clipboard

6 Tap on this button to access the **Gboard** settings

7 Tap on this button to access more options for the Suggestion strip

8 The additional options include: adding a **Theme** to a message; using the keyboard **One-handed**; **Text Editing**; **Share Gboard** with someone else; **Translate**; and **Floating**, which enables the keyboard to be moved around the screen

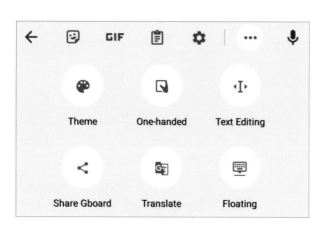

103

Hot tip

If the **One-handed** option is selected in Step 8, the keyboard moves to the left or the right of the screen so that it can more easily be accessed using just one hand.

Don't forget

For some items on the Suggestion strip, such as **Translate**, an item of text has to be selected for it to be active.

General Keyboard Shortcuts

Because of the size of the keyboard on an Android phone, some keys have duplicate functionality, in order to fit in all of the options. This includes dual function keys, spacebar shortcuts and accented letters.

Much of this functionality is accessed by pressing and holding on the keys, rather than just tapping on them once.

Dual functions

If a key has more than one character, both items can be accessed from the same button.

Hot tip

Press and hold on compatible letters on the keyboard to access accented versions for different languages. These include the a, c, e, i, o, s and u keys.

1 Press and hold on the period/full stop key to view additional options. Slide your finger over the character, to insert it

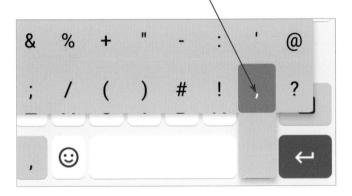

Spacebar shortcut

The spacebar can also be used for a useful shortcut: at the end of a

sentence, double-tap on the spacebar to add a full stop/period and a space, ready for the start of the next sentence, if this is enabled as shown in Step 9 on page 101.

The end.

Adding Text

Once you have applied the keyboard settings that you require, you can start entering text, in appropriate apps.

1 Tap once in a text box to activate the keyboard. Start typing with the keyboard. Text will appear at the point where you tapped on the screen

2 If **Show suggestion strip** is enabled, suggestions appear above the keyboard as you type a word. Tap once on a word on the suggestions strip to include it

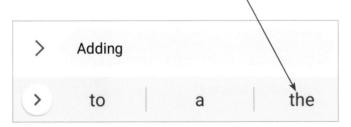

3 If **Next-word suggestions** is enabled, suggestions appear after the last word entered

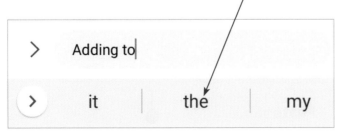

Use the back-delete button to remove unwanted text once it has been added.

If **Show suggestion strip** is enabled in the keyboard settings (see page 101), **Next-word suggestions** is automatically enabled.

For details about adding text to a text message, see pages 108-109.

Working with Text

Once text has been entered it can be selected, copied, cut and pasted, either within an app or between apps.

Selecting text

To select text and perform tasks on it:

1 Tap anywhere to set the insertion point for adding or editing text

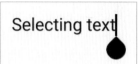

2 Drag the marker to move the insertion point

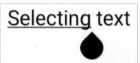

3 Double-tap or press and hold on a word to select it and activate the selection handles

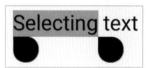

4 Drag the handles to change text that is selected

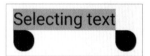

To select all of the text in a text box, press and hold on the text, then tap on the **Select all** button in Step 6.

5 Tap on these options to cut or copy selected text

6 Locate the point at which you want to insert text, and press and hold. Tap on **Paste** to add the text

Messaging and Email

This chapter shows how to keep in touch using text messages, and how to enhance them with emojis and attachments.

Hot tip

When you send a text message to someone, this starts a conversation thread. To delete a thread, in the **Messages** app, press and hold on the conversation thread, and tap on the **Delete** option at the bottom of the window.

Delete

Don't forget

Apps such as WhatsApp and Messenger (Facebook) can be used for texting people. This is known as "internet messaging", and one of its useful features is being able to create text groups so that everyone in a group can see what the other members are saying. It is usually free to message people with these apps.

Texting Contacts

As with phone calls, it is possible to use your contacts to send text messages in a number of ways.

Finding a contact in Messages
To text a contact directly from the Messages app:

1 Tap on the **Messages** app

Messages

2 Tap on this button

3 Enter details of a recipient, or tap on the **+** button to add them from the **Contacts** app

< New conversation

Recipient ⊕

4 The selected contact is added as the recipient of the message

< Select recipients

Search Contacts or enter number

E   Eilidh

5 Enter text for the message

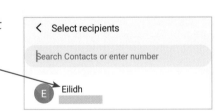

>   Hi, how's it going?

6 Compose the text and tap on this button to send the message

Texting from your Contacts list

You can also text a contact directly from your Contacts list:

1 Tap on the **Contacts** app

2 Find the contact you want to text

3 Tap on the contact's name and tap on the **Message** icon. A new text message is opened with the contact's name already inserted

To call a contact instead of sending them a text, tap on the **Call** button (to the left of the **Message** button), or the **Video call** button if you want to make a video call.

Quick contact messaging

As with a phone call, it is possible to quickly start a text message with a contact with one swipe. To do this:

1 Tap on the **Contacts** app

2 Find the contact you want to text

3 Swipe to the left on the contact's name. An orange **Message** button appears and opens up a new text message with the contact's name already inserted as the recipient

When you are accessing a contact's details by tapping on their name, be careful not to swipe the button instead, as this could activate the quick messaging or calling function by mistake.

Beware

Use emojis sparingly, as the novelty can soon wear off for the recipient.

Beware

Emojis can also be added to emails and any apps where the emoji keyboard is available.

Using Emojis

Emojis (small graphical symbols) are now a common sight in text messages and on social media. Some people love them while others loathe them, but they are now a regular feature in digital communications.

Emojis can be inserted directly from the **Messages** text box.

1 Compose a text message, and at any point, tap on the emoji symbol on the keyboard

2 The default category of emojis is displayed. Tap on an item to add it to a message

3 Tap on this button to view the most recently used emoji

4 Tap on the buttons on the top toolbar to view the emojis' different categories

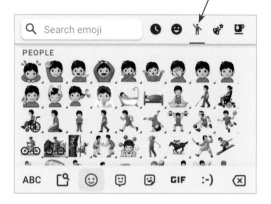

The range of emojis on the Gboard app has been updated for Android 10.

5 Swipe left and right, or tap on the buttons above the emojis, to view the emojis in a category. Tap on an emoji to add it

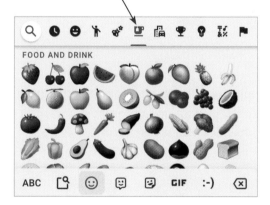

Don't forget

The functionality in Step 6 can be activated by turning **On** the **Show emoji suggestions** option in the **Emoji, Stickers & GIFs** section of the keyboard settings. See page 100 for details.

6 When writing a message, emojis will appear on the shortcuts bar when they match a word that has been entered. Tap on an emoji to replace the word

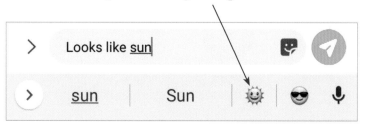

Adding Attachments

Text messages do not have to only include words; it is also possible to attach a variety of other items, such as photos, music tracks and videos.

Beware

If a photo or video is too large to be sent by text, you will see a message saying that it will be compressed before it can be sent.

Beware

A text with attachments such as photos, music tracks and videos may be converted to a multimedia message and may cost more than a regular text, depending on your data contract.

1 Open a new text message and tap on this button next to the text box

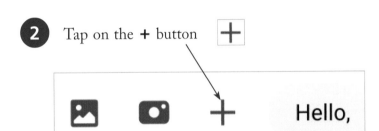

2 Tap on the **+** button

3 Tap on the item to be added – e.g. a map location, an image or a video. The item is included with the text message when it is sent

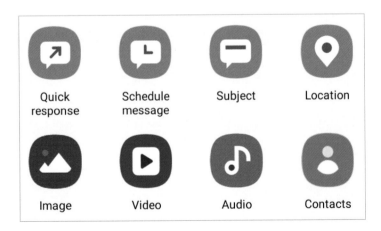

Glide Typing

Another way of creating texts with the Google keyboard is with the **Glide typing** option. This is where you swipe over the keyboard to create words, rather than tapping on individual letters. To do this:

1 Select **Settings > General management > Language and input > On-screen keyboard > Gboard** and tap on **Glide typing**

2 Drag the **Enable glide typing** and **Show gesture trail** buttons **On**

3 When you create a message, drag over the keyboard with a finger to add letters for words you want to create. If the **Show gesture trail** option in Step 2 is **On**, a colored line is visible as your finger moves over the letters. If you need to create a double letter, make a circular motion on the relevant letter on the keyboard

Beware

Glide typing is best used for short messages, rather than trying to write anything of length.

Setting Up Email

Email is still one of the main forms of electronic communication. Most Android phone manufacturers include their own email app for adding email accounts, but the **Gmail** app can also be used for this, in addition to being used for emails from a Google Account. To add an email account:

Don't forget

Email accounts can also be set up from the **Settings** app, under **Accounts and backup** > **Accounts** > **Add account**.

1 Tap on the **Gmail** app

2 Tap on the Gmail **Menu** button in the top left-hand corner

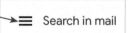

3 Swipe down the menu and tap on the **Settings** button

Hot tip

Usually, email providers have their own apps – e.g. **Microsoft Outlook** for Microsoft accounts; **Yahoo Mail** for Yahoo accounts; etc.

4 Tap on the **Add account** option to add a new account that can be used with the Gmail app

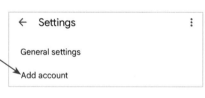

5 Tap on the type of account that you want to add. Tap on the **Other** option if your email account provider is not on the list

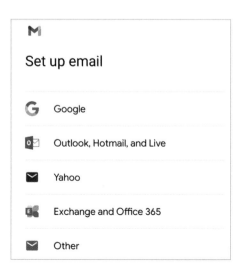

6 Enter the email address of the account you want to add, and then tap on the **Next** button

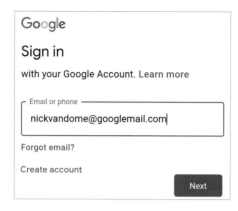

Google

Sign in

with your Google Account. Learn more

Email or phone

nickvandome@googlemail.com

Forgot email?

Create account   Next

Don't forget

Numerous email accounts can be added to the Gmail app.

7 Enter the password for the account you want to add, and then tap on the **Next** button

Google

Hi Nick

👤 nickvandome@googlemail.com

Enter your password

••••••••

☐ Show password

Forgot password?   Next

Don't forget

115

When an email account is synced, any items that are saved online are copied to the phone so that the two locations display the same information.

8 Select options for the account, including those for notifications when emails arrive; syncing the account; and downloading attachments. Tap on the **Accept** button to finish setting up the new account

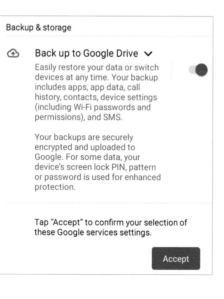

Backup & storage

☁ **Back up to Google Drive** ⌄   ⚫

Easily restore your data or switch devices at any time. Your backup includes apps, app data, call history, contacts, device settings (including Wi-Fi passwords and permissions), and SMS.

Your backups are securely encrypted and uploaded to Google. For some data, your device's screen lock PIN, pattern or password is used for enhanced protection.

Tap "Accept" to confirm your selection of these Google services settings.

Accept

Using Gmail

Accessing emails

Emails from different email accounts can all be viewed and managed using Gmail. To do this:

1 Tap on the **Gmail** app

2 By default, Gmail should open at your Inbox, with your emails displayed. Tap on one to open it. Tap on the **Menu** button to view the mailbox options

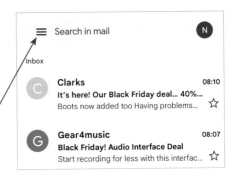

3 Tap on the **Inbox** button to return to your Inbox at any point. Tap on the other options to view folders with specific items, such as **Sent** mail and any **Drafts** you have written

4 Tap on the **All mail** option to view emails from multiple accounts, if more than one has been added to Gmail

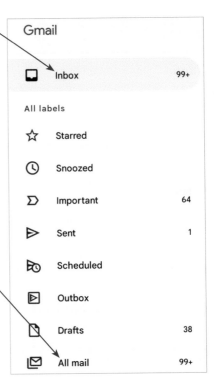

Creating an email

Once you have set up an email account, you can use it to send and receive all of your emails on your Android phone. To send an email:

1 Tap on the **Gmail** app

2 Tap on the **Compose** button

3 Compose the email by adding a recipient, subject and body text

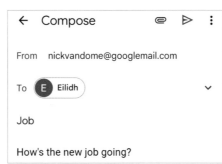

117

4 To format text, press on a word to select it. Tap on the **Format** button to access the formatting toolbar

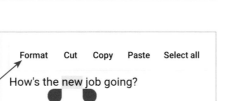

5 Choose the required formatting for the selected word, including bold, italics, underlining, text color, background text color and strikethrough

6 When you have finished composing your email, tap on this button to send it

Going Hands-free

If you do not want to bother fiddling around with fingers and thumbs to create your messages, you can use **Speech** mode instead.

1 Open a new text message or email and tap on the microphone icon

2 When the **Speak now** window appears, speak your message as clearly as possible

3 As you are speaking, the **Listening...** window appears

4 Your words will be converted into text

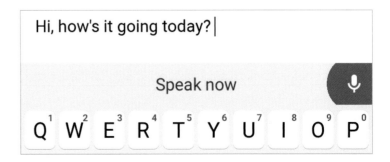

Beware

Creating text with the microphone is not an exact science and you may find that you end up with some strange interpretations of your words.

8 Android Apps

The functionality on an Android phone is provided by its apps. This chapter details the pre-installed ones, and shows how to download more and update them. It also looks at some of the most common apps, covering maps, notes, social media, health and fitness, and games.

Apps for Android

An app is just a more modern name for a computer program. The terminology first became widely used on smartphones, but has now spread to all forms of computing and is firmly embedded in the language of phones.

On Android phones there are three main types of apps:

- **Generic apps** – Come pre-installed on your Android phone. In general, these apps are specific to the manufacturer of the phone.

- **Google apps** – Downloaded from the online Play Store. Google apps are compatible with the same apps on other Google devices. A number of these apps are also pre-installed on a lot of Android phones.

- **Apps from other developers** – Non-Google apps, downloaded from the Play Store.

Generic apps

The types of generic apps that are available on Android phones include:

- **Calculator**. A standard calculator that also has some scientific functions, although not the range of a full scientific calculator.

Calculator

- **Calendar**. An app for storing appointments, important dates and other calendar information.

Calendar

- **Camera**. Android smartphones have at least one camera and most have two: a front-facing and back-facing one. These can be accessed from the **Camera** app.

Camera

- **Clock**. This can be used to view the time in different countries, and also functions as an alarm clock, a timer, and a stopwatch.

Clock

Don't forget

Because of the open source nature of Android, manufacturers can customize the built-in apps for their devices.

Don't forget

Most apps have menu options that can be accessed from the buttons below (some apps have both, but they provide the same menu functionality):

120

- **Contacts.** The **Contacts** app serves as an address book where you can enter details about your friends and family members. Calls and texts can be sent directly from the app.

Contacts

- **Internet.** Although a generic internet app is included with a lot of Android phones, the **Google Chrome** app is probably the best option for accessing the web.

Internet

Don't forget

Health and fitness apps record details including number of steps taken, calories consumed, heart rate, and workout activity. See page 128 for details.

- **Messages.** This is the generic app for sending text messages, which is done through your 3G/4G/5G cellular network.

Messages

- **Phone.** This is the generic app for making calls (and accessing contacts for calls) and video calls.

Phone

- **Gallery.** In addition to the **Camera** app, some Android phones have a **Gallery** app that can be used to view, manage, edit and share photos, and other models feature a **Photos** app, which serves the same purpose.

Gallery

- **Play Store.** Although this is a Google app, it is included on most Android phones so that you can access the Play Store for downloading apps, books, music, movies and magazines.

Play Store

Don't forget

In addition to the Play Store, some phone manufacturers also offer their own app stores, although the range of apps is usually more limited.

- **Notes/Memos.** Notes and memo apps are provided on most Android phones, and they are useful for jotting down items such as shopping lists and packing lists for traveling.

Notes

- **Settings.** This contains all of the settings that can be applied to the phone so that you can customize it the way you want.

Settings

121

Google Apps

Most Android phones come with some Google apps already pre-installed. If not, the apps can be downloaded from the Play Store. The Google apps for Android phones include:

- **Assistant**. This is Google's app for searching for items by speaking. Tap on the app and then speak your search query.

- **Chrome**. Different Android phones have different types of browsers for accessing the web. The Chrome browser is the default on some phones.

- **Docs**. This can be used to create word processing documents and keep them in cloud storage (online storage) or on your phone.

- **Drive**. This app provides online storage and backup for documents and files on your phone, stored by Google.

- **Duo**. This is Google's app for making video calls, using your Google Account and your device's camera.

- **Gmail**. When you set up a Google Account you will also create a Gmail account for sending and receiving email. This app can be used for accessing and using your Gmail.

- **Google**. This app can be used for accessing the **Google Search** function – still one of the best search facilities available. It can also be used for accessing the **Google Discover** function.

- **Google TV**. Google TV has replaced the **Google Play Movies & TV** app and offers a huge range of movies and TV shows.

The range of Google apps has been updated in Android 10, to include the Google TV and the YT Music app.

...cont'd

- **Maps**. The Google Maps app is one of the best mapping apps available for finding locations and obtaining directions.

- **News**. This is a news app that collates stories on specific topics, or from certain publications.

Some Android phones have different apps for functions such as playing music and movies, and reading books and magazines. If this is the case, the Play apps here can still be downloaded from the Play Store.

- **Play Books**. This is the app for reading ebooks on an Android phone. It can be used to manage books in your library and also download new ones from the Play Store.

- **Play Games**. This is the app for accessing games from the Play Store and playing them on your phone.

- **Sheets**. This can be used to create spreadsheets and keep them in cloud storage (online storage) or on your phone.

- **Slides**. This can be used to create presentations and keep them in cloud storage (online storage) or on your phone.

- **YouTube**. This is the popular video-sharing app that is now owned by Google. It can be used to view millions of videos covering most subjects imaginable.

- **YT Music**. **YouTube Music** (**YT Music**) has replaced the **Play Music** app that was previously available on Android smartphones. A huge range of music can be accessed from here.

Maps

The default maps app on Android phones is **Google Maps**, one of the best mapping apps on the market. It can be used to view locations, get directions and view transit details.

Don't forget

When viewing a map in Step 2, tap on this button to view your current location at any point:

1   Tap on the **Maps** app

2   The current location is displayed (if **Location** is enabled under **Settings > Location**). Double-tap with one finger to zoom in; double-tap with two fingers to zoom out. Swipe outward with thumb and forefinger to zoom in; pinch inward to zoom out

3   To view other locations, type a place name, address, zip/postcode or landmark in the Search box at the top of the window. Results are displayed as you type

4   Tap on one of the results to view a map of it. Some locations also have additional features such as photos. Tap on an item to view it, or swipe up from the bottom of the window to view more details about a location and questions that have been asked about it

Getting directions

The **Maps** app is very effective in providing directions between two points. To do this:

1. Tap on the **Directions** button

2. Enter the starting point and destination for the directions in the text fields at the top of the window (by default, the starting point is your current location but this can be changed by tapping in the field and entering a new location for the starting point). The route is displayed on the map. Tap the **Menu** button to add a stop, and for more options

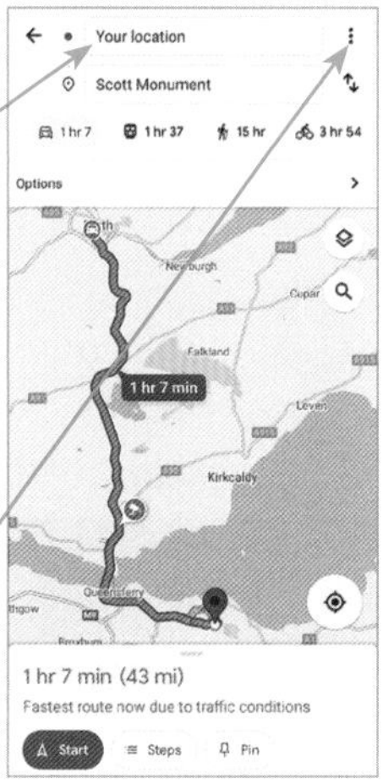

3. Tap on these buttons to select the mode of transport for the journey

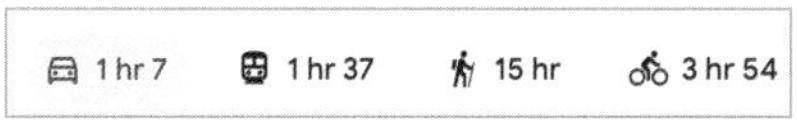

4. Tap on the **Start** button to view step-by-step directions for the journey

5. As you change your location the map updates accordingly and gives you spoken directions. Tap the **Speaker** button for options to turn off spoken directions (mute) or to hear alerts only

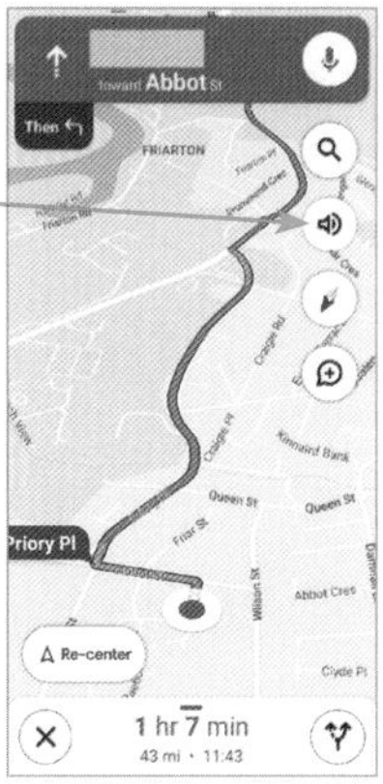

Tap on the **Menu** button on the top toolbar, when viewing a location on a map, to access options such as adding the route to the Home screen and sharing your location.

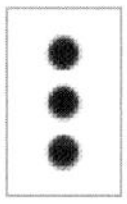

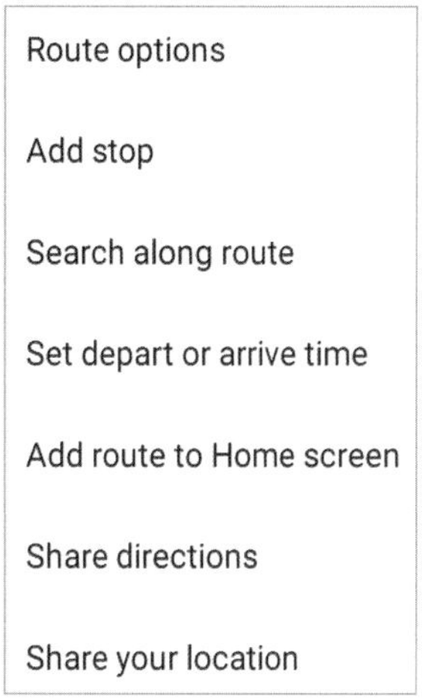

Notes and Memos

Taking notes on an Android phone is an excellent way to keep up-to-date with a range of tasks, from shopping lists to reminders for packing for a trip. There are several notes and memos apps that can be downloaded from the Play Store, and most smartphone manufacturers include default notes and memos apps. The example here uses the **Notes** app. To use it:

Hot tip

Lists with checklists is a great option for feeling productive, when you can see all of the items that have been completed.

1 Tap on the **Notes** app

2 Tap on this button to create a new note

3 Tap on the **Create checklist** option for a list or tap on the **Create note** option to add a note

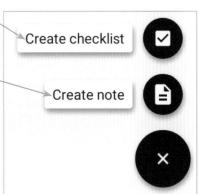

4 Enter the content for the note and tap on the back arrow to go back to a panel with all of your notes

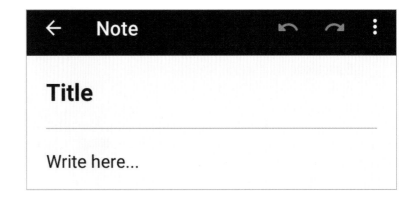

Social Media

Social media has transformed the way in which we communicate, and there are numerous apps that can be used on an Android phone for social media. These can be downloaded from the Play Store, from within the **Social** category. Some of the most popular apps are:

Facebook

This is still one of the most widely used social media tools. To use Facebook you have to first register, which is free. You can then link up with your friends and share a variety of content, by searching for them and inviting them to join your network with a Friend Request.

Twitter

Twitter is a microblogging site where users post short messages (tweets). Once you have joined Twitter, which is free, you can follow other users to see what they are saying and have people follow you too.

Snapchat

Snapchat is a messaging service that allows users to send photos and videos to their Snapchat friends, or groups of people. Once these are accessed, they remain visible for a few seconds and then they are deleted. Text and graphics can be added to items when they are sent – one of the most frequent uses is for sending self-portraits ("selfies" – see page 156).

Pinterest

This is an online pinboard, where you can bookmark and "pin" items of interest and upload your own content for other people to pin.

Instagram

This is a popular photo- and video-sharing site. Followers can be added by users and they can then comment and "like" photos. By default, the security settings are for public viewing of content, so these should be changed if you only want your own followers to be able to view your content.

Don't forget

YouTube is one of the great successes of the internet age. It is a video-sharing site, with millions of video clips covering every subject imaginable. There is a built-in YouTube app on most Android phones that can be accessed from the **All Apps** button.

Health and Fitness

Monitoring health and fitness with digital devices is a growth industry, and there is also a range of health and fitness apps that can record exercise activity on your Android phone. One of these is the **Google Fit** app. To use this:

1 Tap on the **Fit** app

2 Tap on this button to enter health and fitness information or start a new activity

3 Select an option from the menu – e.g. **Add activity**. This can be used for entering data for an activity that you have already undertaken

4 Select the type of activity that you want to record, and tap on the **Save** button

5 If **Track workout** is selected in Step 3, tap on the **Start** button to begin recording the workout activity. Tap on the **Pause** button to pause the workout recording

Playing Games

Although computer games may seem like the preserve of the younger generation, this is definitely not the case. Not all computer games are of the shoot-em-up or racing variety, and the Play Store also contains puzzles and versions of popular board games. Some games to try are:

- **Chess**. Pit your wits against this Chess app. Various settings can be applied for each game, such as the level of difficulty.

- **Checkers**. Similar to the Chess app, but for Checkers (Draughts). Hints are also available to help develop your skills and knowledge.

- **Mahjong**. A version of the popular Chinese game, this is a matching game for single players, rather than playing with other people.

- **Scrabble**. An Android phone version of the best-selling word game that can be played with up to four people.

- **Solitaire**. An old favorite, the card game where you have to build sequences and remove all of the cards.

- **Sudoku**. The logic game where you have to fill different grids with numbers 1-9, without having any of the same number in a row or column.

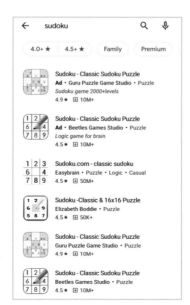

- **Tetris**. One of the original computer games, where you have to piece together falling shapes to make lines.

- **Words With Friends**. Similar to Scrabble, an online word game, played with other users.

Don't forget

As well as the games here, there is a full range of other types of games in the Play Store, which can be accessed from the **Games** category. They can also be accessed from the **Play Games** app.

Play Games

Around the Play Store

Although the pre-installed apps provide a lot of useful functionality and are a good starting point, the Play Store is where you can really start to take advantage of the wide range of apps that are available. These can be used for entertainment, communication, productivity and much more.

To access the Play Store and find apps:

Don't forget

New apps are added to the Play Store on a regular basis (and existing ones are updated), so the Homepage will change appearance regularly.

Don't forget

App prices are shown in the local currency.

1 Tap on the **Play Store** app

2 Suggested items are shown on the Play Store Homepage, under the **For you** tab

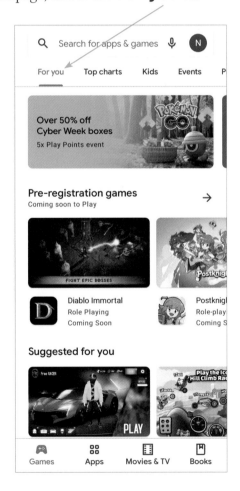

3 Swipe up and down or left and right to see the full range of recommendations for all types of content in the Play Store. Tap on an item to view further details about it

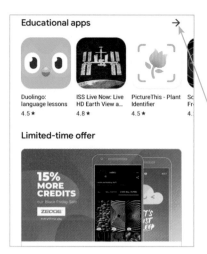

Tap on this button from a section on the Homepage to view additional items.

4 Use these buttons on the bottom toolbar to find relevant content: **Games**, **Apps**, **Movies & TV** and **Books**

5 Tap on the **Account** button to access the Play Store menu

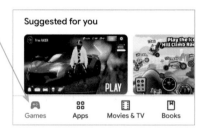

Finding Apps

Searching by category

When you have accessed the Play Store you can then look for content in a variety of ways.

There may be different apps available in the Play Store, depending on your geographical location.

1 The featured and recommended items are displayed on the Homepage (by default, this opens on the **Games** section). Swipe up and down and left and right to view the full range, and tap on an item to view more details

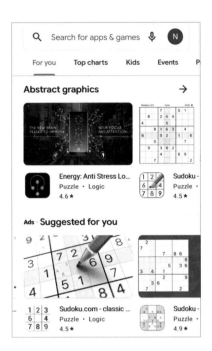

2 Tap on the **Apps** button on the bottom toolbar to view the available range of apps. Swipe left and right on the top bar to view apps according to **For You**, **Top Charts**, **Events**, **Kids**, **Categories**, and **Editors' Choice**

Apps

3 Tap on the **Categories** tab in Step 2 on the previous page, and tap on a category to view apps according to the relevant headings

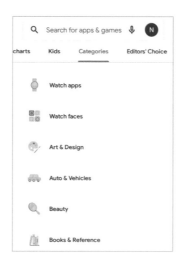

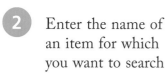

4 Search for apps within a category in the same way as for searching over a whole range of apps, as in Step 2 on the previous page

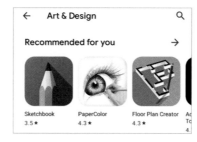

Using the Search box

1 Tap in the **Google Play** Search box on any page to conduct a search with keywords

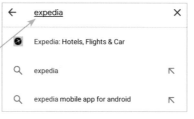

2 Enter the name of an item for which you want to search

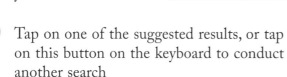

3 Tap on one of the suggested results, or tap on this button on the keyboard to conduct another search

Don't forget

As you type in the Search box, the suggested items will change, depending on the keyword(s) used.

Downloading Apps

Once you have found an app in the Play Store that you want to use, you can download it to your phone.

Hot tip

If you have a phone with 3G/4G/5G cellular capability, try downloading apps over Wi-Fi to avoid using too much of your data allowance.

Don't forget

If an app has a price button on it, you will need to add credit/debit card details to your Google Account. This can be done when the account is set up, or from the Play Store menu (**Payment methods**).

Hot tip

Under **Settings** > **Apps**, select apps to apply settings for their notifications in the Notification panel.

1 Access the app you want to use. There will be details about the app and reviews from other users if you scroll down the page

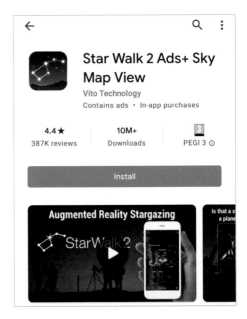

2 Tap on the **Install** button, and the app will start downloading

3 Tap on the **Open** button to open the app once it has finished downloading and installing

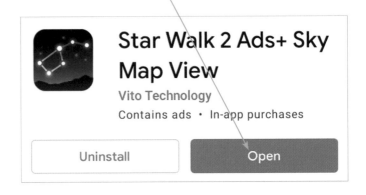

4 Some apps will ask to use your location, to improve their functionality. Select one of the options, as required, for giving permission for this

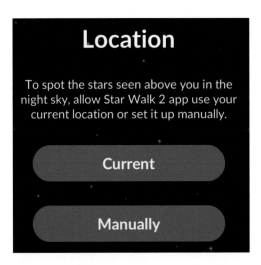

If an app has access to your device's location, it creates more location-specific content. If you deny an app permissions, it may not work.

5 Tap on the **Allow** or **Deny** options, as required, to give access to your location, or not, as selected in Step 4

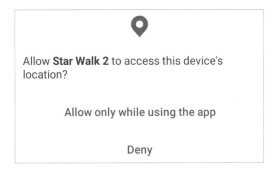

6 Newly downloaded apps usually appear on the next available **All Apps** screen where there is a space. From here, the app can be opened and also moved to another location. A shortcut on your Home screen is sometimes also created

Uninstalling Apps

The pre-installed apps on an Android phone cannot be deleted easily (although they can be turned off), but the ones that have been downloaded from the Play Store can be uninstalled. You may want to do this if you do not use a certain app any more or you feel the number of apps on your phone is becoming too great. To uninstall a downloaded app:

The process for uninstalling apps has been updated in Android 10.

1 Access the **All Apps** section, or the Home screen, then press on an app and tap on the **Uninstall** button

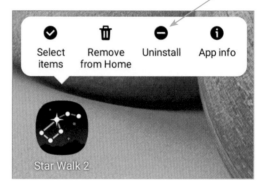

2 Tap on the **OK** button to confirm the uninstall

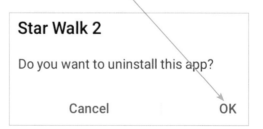

If apps have been uninstalled from the phone, they can be reinstalled from the Play Store app by tapping on your **Account** icon. Tap on the **Manage apps & device** option and tap on the **Manage** tab to view all of the apps that have previously been downloaded.

3 Tap on the **Select items** button in Step 1 to select more than one app. Tap on the **Uninstall** button to uninstall the selected apps

Turning off built-in apps

Pre-installed apps cannot be uninstalled easily, but they can be turned off so that they cannot be used. This is done in a similar way to uninstalling apps.

1 Press and hold the app to be turned off. Tap on the **Disable** button

2 A warning will appear, alerting you to the fact that you are disabling the app. Tap on the **Disable** button to continue

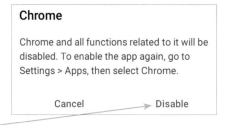

Chrome

Chrome and all functions related to it will be disabled. To enable the app again, go to Settings > Apps, then select Chrome.

Cancel   → Disable

3 To turn the app back on, access **Settings** > **Apps** and tap on the turned-off app

Chrome
47.00 MB
Disabled

4 Tap on the **Turn on** button to turn the app back on

Turn on   Force stop

Beware

Phone manufacturers can add their own apps to Android phones and, in some cases, it is not possible to either uninstall or turn off these apps.

137

Updating Apps

The world of apps is a dynamic and fast-moving one, and new apps are being created and added to the Play Store on a daily basis. Existing apps are also updated, to improve their performance and functionality. These can be added to your phone either automatically or manually.

Updating apps automatically

Apps are also updated to improve security features and include any fixes to improve the performance of the app.

1 Access the Play Store. Tap on the **Account** button and then the **Settings** button

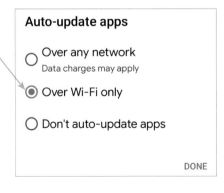

2 Tap on the **Network preferences** option and tap on the **Auto-update apps** option

Some app updates will require your confirmation before updating, even if you have chosen to auto-update apps.

3 Tap on the **Over Wi-Fi only** radio button so that it contains a colored dot. Available updates will be installed automatically when the phone is connected to Wi-Fi

Updating apps manually
Apps can also be updated manually.

1 Ensure **Don't auto-update apps** is selected in Step 3 on the previous page

Don't auto-update apps

DONE

2 Access the Play Store. Tap on the **Account** button and then the **Manage apps & device** option

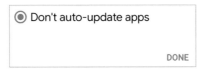

Beware

If apps are set to be updated manually, check regularly in the Play Store to see if there are any updates that you want to install for your apps.

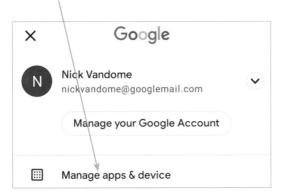

×   Google

N   Nick Vandome
nickvandome@googlemail.com   ⌄

Manage your Google Account

▦   Manage apps & device

3 Tap on the **Overview** tab and on the **Update all** option to apply all of the available updates. Tap on the **See details** option to view information about the updates and update them individually

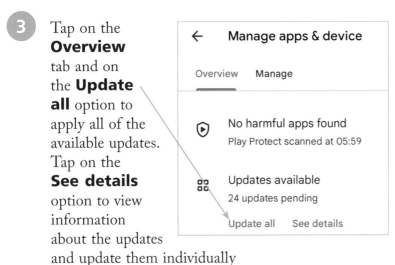

←   Manage apps & device

Overview   Manage

⊳   No harmful apps found
Play Protect scanned at 05:59

⊞   Updates available
24 updates pending

Update all   See details

App Information

For both pre-installed apps and those downloaded from the Play Store, it is possible to view details about them and also see the permissions that they are using to access certain functions. To view information about your apps:

1 Open the **Settings** app and tap on the **Apps** button

2 Tap on an app to select it and view its details

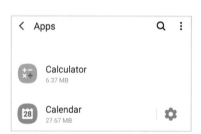

Don't forget

Tap on the **Notifications** button in the **App info** window in Step 3 to specify how notifications are handled for the app. Drag the **Show notifications** button **On** to enable notifications to be displayed for the app.

3 Tap on the **Mobile data** option to view details about the size of the app, and the amount of data it has stored

4 Tap on the **Force stop** button on the bottom toolbar to close a running app

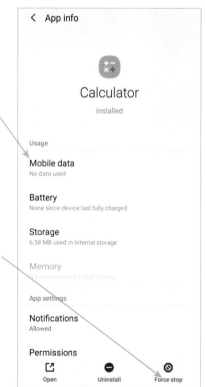

9 Being Entertained

This chapter shows how to use your phone for playing music, watching movies and reading books.

The Google Play Website

Google Play is Google's online store for buying, downloading, using and managing a range of entertainment content. It is accessed at the following website:

- **play.google.com**

For details about opening web pages, see page 169.

You need to have a Google Account in order to log in to the Google Play website. Once you have logged in to Google Play you can download a variety of content:

- Movies and TV shows

- Audiobooks

- Ebooks

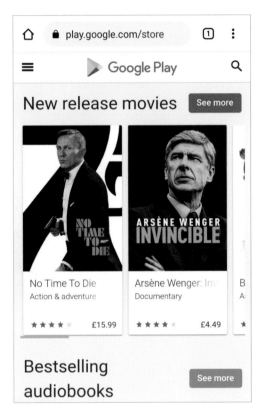

Content that is downloaded to your Android phone via the Play Store will also be available on the Google Play website, as long as you are logged in with your Google Account.

Content from Google Play is stored in the cloud so that it can then be used on your computer and also your Android phone. If you delete it from your phone, either accidentally or on purpose, you can still reinstall it from Google Play. You can also use content downloaded by any of your other Android devices, such as a tablet.

The **YT Music** app, the **Google TV** app and the **Play Books** app can also be used to access music, movies and TV shows, and ebooks and audiobooks, respectively. See the next 12 pages for details about using these apps.

Music on Android

The options for accessing and playing music on smartphones with Android 10 have been updated through the use of the **YT Music** app, which has replaced the **Play Music** app. This provides access to Google's huge catalog of music, much of which can be played for free on your Android smartphone. To use the **YT Music** app:

1 Tap on the **YT Music** app

YT Music

The **YT Music** app is a new feature in Android 10. YT stands for YouTube.

2 Select five of your favorite artists from the first window. This will help the **YT Music** app tailor future suggestions and recommendation to your tastes

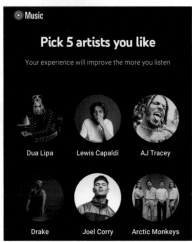

3 The **YT Music** app opens at the Homepage, which can also be accessed from the **Home** button on the bottom toolbar. Swipe along the top toolbar and tap on the categories to view their content

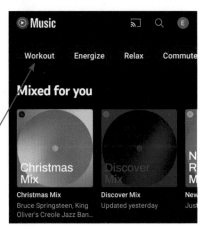

...cont'd

4 Swipe down the Homepage to view the rest of its content, and also access radio stations, based on song selections

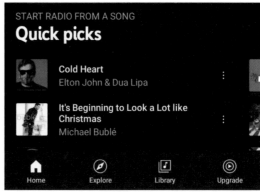

Hot tip

Tap on the **Search** icon at the top of the **YT Music** app to search for artists and tracks. Artists are listed with tracks, albums, playlists and artists with which they have collaborated.

5 Tap on the **Explore** button on the bottom toolbar, to view the latest available music and suggested items

Explore

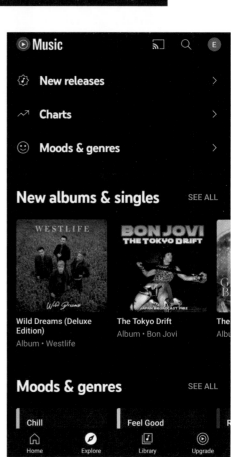

6 Tap on the **Library** button on the bottom toolbar to view items that you have viewed or played. Tap on an item to view more details about it

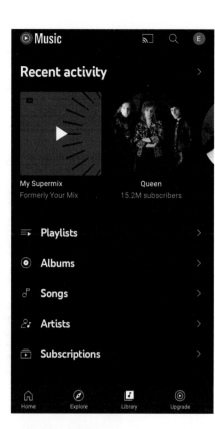

Hot tip

Tap on the **Upgrade** button on the bottom toolbar in Step 6 to upgrade to the **Music Premium** service, which is advert-free, provides a greater range of music and allows you to download music so that you can listen to it when you are offline and not connected to the internet.

7 Select an artist, or album, to view related tracks. Tap on a track to play it, or tap on the **Play** button to play a whole album, or a playlist

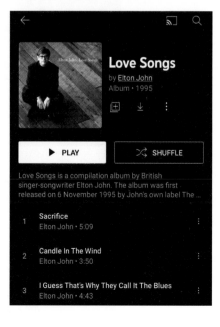

...cont'd

8 When a track is tapped on, it opens in its own music window, with music controls for the track. Tap here to minimize the music window so that you can continue exploring in the **YT Music** app, while the track is playing

Hot tip

Tap on the **Menu** button in the top right-hand corner of the window in Step 8 to access options for the current item being played.

((·)) Start radio

≡▶ Play next

≡♪ Add to queue

⊞ Add to library

↓ Download

≡+ Add to playlist

◉ Go to album

♀♪ Go to artist

↷ Share

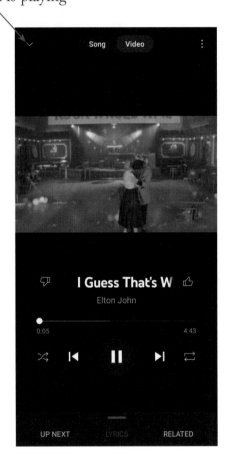

9 Use the music controls to, from left to right: shuffle tracks; go to the start of a track; pause or play a track; go to the end of a track; and repeat a track

Google TV

The **Google TV** app is a new way of watching movies and TV shows on your Android smartphone. It offers a significant range of content, including from different providers, such as Disney+ and Amazon Prime. Content is streamed to your Android smartphone by default, which means it is played on your device without being downloaded onto it. To use the **Google TV** app:

1 Tap on the **Google TV** app

2 The **Google TV** app opens at the **For you** page, on the **Home** page, which consists of recommended movies and TV shows

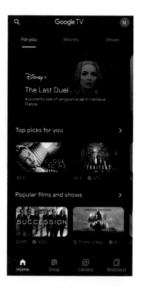

The **Google TV** app is a new feature in Android 10.

3 Swipe down the page to view the full range of content that is available

…cont'd

Don't forget

For items that require a subscription to a third-party streaming service, tap on the relevant **Subscribe** button and sign up for the service.

4 Tap on the **Movies** tab on the top toolbar to view a range of available movies

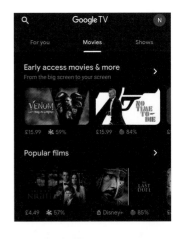

5 Tap on the **Shows** tab on the top toolbar to view a range of available TV shows

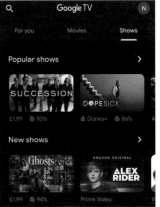

6 Tap on the **Shop** button on the bottom toolbar to view items that you can buy from Google TV

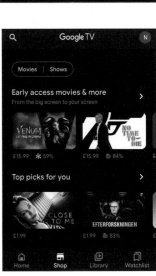

7 Tap on the arrow next to a category to view its full range of content

8 Swipe down the page to view the full range of content that is on offer. Tap on an item to view its details

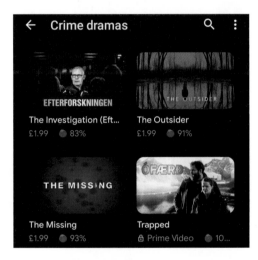

9 Tap on the **Library** button on the bottom toolbar to view items that you have bought or downloaded from Google TV

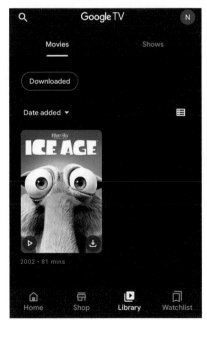

Rented items will be removed from the Library once the rental period expires.

Some phones have their own default movies app, which will be linked to the phone manufacturer's own app store. If this is the case, the **Play Movies** app can still be downloaded from the Play Store, and content can be bought from there.

When buying or renting items from the Play Store, there are usually options for doing so in Standard Definition (SD) or High Definition (HD).

Movies and TV Shows

Although the **Google TV** app has replaced the **Play Movies & TV** app, this range of content can also be obtained through the **Movies & TV** section in the Play Store. From here, movies and TV shows can be bought or downloaded. To obtain movies or TV shows from the Play Store:

1 Tap on the **Play Store** app

2 Tap on the **Movies & TV** button on the bottom toolbar to view available content on your phone. This includes movies and TV shows that you have downloaded, and also any recommended titles

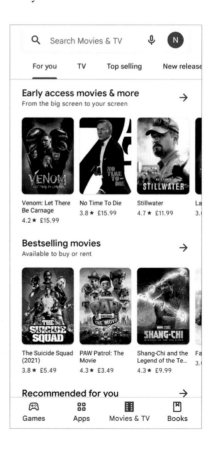

3 Tap on these buttons to buy or rent a movie or TV show. This will be made available within the **Google TV** app. (If you rent a movie or a TV show it has to be started within 30 days of being rented, and watched within 48 hours of when it was first started)

Tap on the Search icon at the top of the **Movies & TV** page to search for specific items, using keywords.

4 Tap on the **TV** button on the top toolbar to access this content

5 Tap on an item to view details about it and watch a preview clip of the item

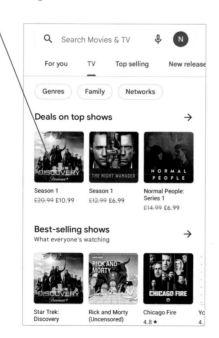

If you download movies and TV shows to your phone, they can take up a considerable amount of storage space. Rented items will be automatically deleted once the rental period expires.

Obtaining Ebooks

Due to their size and portability, Android phones are often used for reading ebooks. There is a wide range that can be downloaded from the Play Store, or from the Google Play website. To do this:

Don't forget

Android phones with larger screens are recommended for reading ebooks.

Don't forget

Swipe left and right on a panel on the **Shop** Homepage to view the items within it.

Hot tip

One of the categories in the **Play Books** store section is for **Top free** ebooks. Some classic titles also have free versions if the copyright has expired after a certain period of time following the author's death.

1 Tap on the **Play Books** app (or access the Google Play website)

Play Books

2 Tap on the **Library** button on the bottom toolbar to view your titles. Tap on a cover to open a specific title

Library

3 Tap on the **Shop** button on the bottom toolbar

Shop

4 Ebooks can be browsed for and downloaded in a similar way as for other Play Store content. Tap on these buttons to view the available categories

5 Tap on a title to view details about it

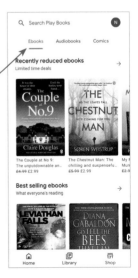

6 When you find an ebook you want to read, tap on the **Free sample** button (if there is one) or the **Buy** button (with the price)

7 When any ebook from the Play Books store has been downloaded to your phone, it is available within your Play Books Library

Hot tip

The **Kindle** app can be downloaded from the Play Store for reading ebooks. If you already have a Kindle account, your ebooks will be available through the **Kindle** app on your phone.

153

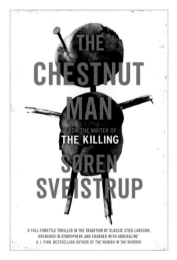

8 Simply select it to open it, and tap in the middle of the page to access the reading controls

Around an Ebook

Once you have downloaded ebooks to your phone, you can start reading them. Due to their format, there is a certain amount of electronic functionality that is not available in a hard copy version. To find your way around an ebook:

You can also move to the next or previous page of an ebook by tapping at the right-hand or left-hand edge of a page.

1 Swipe left and right on a page to move backward or forward by one page

2 Tap in the middle of a page to access the reading controls toolbars at the top and bottom of the screen

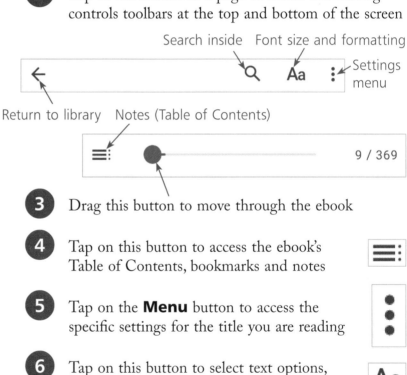

Search inside   Font size and formatting

Settings menu

Return to library   Notes (Table of Contents)

9 / 369

3 Drag this button to move through the ebook

4 Tap on this button to access the ebook's Table of Contents, bookmarks and notes

5 Tap on the **Menu** button to access the specific settings for the title you are reading

6 Tap on this button to select text options, including font size and line height

Aa

7 Tap in the top right-hand corner of a page to add a bookmark. A blue bookmark icon appears. Tap again to remove it. Tap on the button in Step 4 to view all bookmarks

1

leaves drift down

10 Keeping in the Picture

This chapter shows how to make the most of the high-quality cameras that come with most Android phones.

Using Cameras

Most Android phones have their own built-in cameras, which can be used to capture photos directly onto the device. The quality of these varies between makes of phone. Some are good-quality cameras intended to be used for taking photos in a range of conditions; others are mainly for use as a webcam for video calls, or for "selfies" (these are front-facing cameras). To use an Android camera phone:

Hot tip

Use the front-facing camera – i.e. the one on the phone's screen – to take "selfies", which are self-portraits that can also include other people.

Don't forget

The most recently captured photo is displayed at the left-hand side of the bottom toolbar. Tap on it to open it in the **Photos** app.

Don't forget

Tap on the **Video** option in Step 2 to record a video rather than take a photo.

1 Tap on the **Camera** app

2 The **Camera** app displays the current scene, and the control buttons are displayed at the side (landscape view) or at the bottom (portrait view)

3 Press on the screen to focus the current scene, and tap on this button to take a photo

4 Tap on this button to switch between the front- and rear-facing cameras

5 Further controls are available at the top of the screen on the shortcuts bar

6 Tap on the buttons above the shutter button to access different shooting modes and filter options. Tap on one of the options to select that for the next photo

By default, photos captured with the Camera app are displayed in the **Photos** or **Gallery** apps.

157

7 Tap on the **Settings** button in Step 5 on the previous page to view the full range of settings for the camera

Different models of Android phones have their own cameras, which include specific settings and modes. However, the ones listed here will be similar across most Android cameras.

8 Tap on one of the items to activate or deactivate it – e.g. the size of photos when they are captured

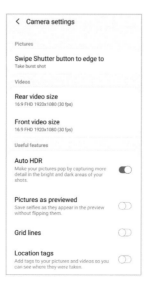

Adding Photos

Android phones are great for storing and, more importantly, displaying your photos. The screen size of most phones is ideal for looking at photos and you can quickly transform it into your own mobile photo album. In addition, it is also possible to share all of your photos in a variety of ways.

Obtaining photos

In addition to capturing photos with your phone, you can obtain them in a number of ways:

- Transferring photos from your computer directly to your phone, via a USB cable (into the **Pictures** folder).

- Transferring photos from your camera to your phone. This is usually done by inserting your camera's memory card into a card reader connected to your computer and then transferring your photos as above.

- Downloading and saving photos from an email, social media, a website or from an internet messaging app.

- Transferring photos from another device via Bluetooth.

Once you have captured or transferred photos to your phone you can then view, edit and share them using the **Photos** (or **Gallery**) app. Photos in the **Photos** app are stored in different albums that are created automatically when photos are taken, transferred, or downloaded from an email.

If you keep a lot of photos on your phone this will start to take up storage space.

Personal videos can also be transferred in the same way as with photos. Copy them into the **Videos** folder of your phone. Videos can also be recorded with the **Video** button in the **Camera** app.

The **Photos** app is a Google app and is available in the Play Store if it is not pre-installed on a phone.

Downloading from email

Email is a good method of obtaining photos on your phone; other people can send their photos to you in this way, and you can also email your own photos from a computer, a tablet or another mobile device. To use photos from email:

1 Open the email containing the photo and tap on this button to download it

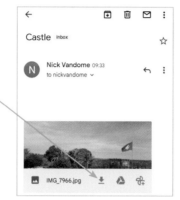

Once the **Download** folder has been created, all other photos downloaded from emails will be placed here.

2 The photo will be saved in the **Download** folder within the **Photos** app. This will be automatically created if it is not already there

3 Tap on the photo to open the album, and tap on it again to view it at full size in the **Photos** app

Viewing Photos

Once you have obtained photos on your Android phone you can start viewing, managing and editing them.

1 Open the **Photos** app and tap on the **Library** button at the bottom of the screen to view the available options within it

Library

The default albums in the **Photos** app are initially empty.

2 Tap on the **View all** option in the **Photos on device** section to view all of the photos on your Android phone

Tap on the **Photos** button at the bottom of the screen to view photos that have been taken with the phone.

Photos

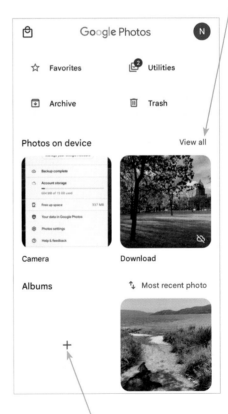

3 Tap here to create a new album for storing photos; see page 163 for details

...cont'd

The photos in the **Photos** app can be worked with and viewed in different ways:

1 Open the **Photos** app and access the **Photos** section as shown on the previous page

Photos

2 The photos and the date on which they were taken are displayed

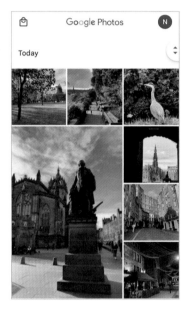

Don't forget

Swipe up the page in Step 2 to view your photos in date order.

3 Tap on a photo to view it at full size

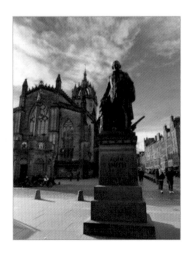

...cont'd

4 Press and hold on photos to select them

Items selected in
Step 5 can be shared
in a variety of ways by
tapping on this button
(see page 166 for
details):

5 Use the toolbar above the image to apply actions
to the selection. These include, from left to right:
sharing the selection; adding the selection to an
album, a movie, an animation or a collage; deleting a
selection; or ordering an online photo book with the
selection

6 Tap on the **Menu** button in Step 5 to access
options for deleting or moving the selection

Delete from device

Move to Archive

Adding Albums

In addition to the pre-inserted device albums, new ones can be added from the **Library** section of the **Photos** app. To do this:

1 Tap on the **Library** button

2 Tap on the **+** button under the **Albums** heading

3 Give the album a name, then tap on the **Select photos** option

4 Tap on the photos to be included in the album and tap on the **Add** button

Add

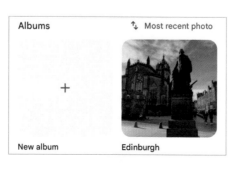

5 The new album is included in the **Albums** section in the **Library**

Individual photos can be added to albums by viewing them at full size, tapping on the **Menu** button as in Step 6 on the previous page, tapping on the **Add to album** option and selecting the required album. Alternatively, select them as in Step 5 on the previous page, tap on the **+** (plus) button on the top toolbar, and select **Create** > **Album**.

Hot tip

Editing Photos

Although the **Photos** app is more for viewing photos, it does have a few editing options so that you can tweak and enhance your images. To access and use these:

1 Tap on a photo to view it. Tap on the **Edit** button on the bottom toolbar to access the editing options

2 Tap on the **Enhance** button to access options for applying quick (one-tap) editing options to the photo

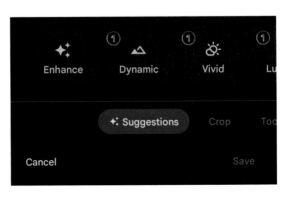

Beware

Add small editing changes at a time, otherwise the effect may look too severe.

...cont'd

3 Swipe along the bottom toolbar and tap on the **Adjust** button to select a range of color-editing functions, including editing the brightness and color contrast of the photo

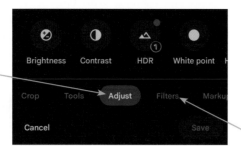

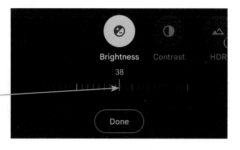

Tap on the **Filters** option in Step 3 to apply colored filters to the photo being edited. Tap on a filter thumbnail to apply it to the photo.

4 Tap on the **Adjust** options to expand them and access sliders for editing elements for the selection

5 To crop a photo, tap on the **Crop** button on the toolbar in Step 3 and drag the resizing handles to crop the photo

6 Tap on this button to rotate the photo manually, clockwise or anti-clockwise

Most photos benefit from some cropping, to give the main subject more prominence.

7 Tap on the **Save** button to save any editing changes that have been made

Sharing Photos

It can be great fun and very rewarding to share photos with friends and family. With an Android phone, this can be done in different ways.

Don't forget

Social networking sites such as Facebook and Twitter are ideal for sharing photos. Their respective apps can be downloaded from the Play Store, in which case they will also appear as one of the sharing options in Step 2 opposite.

Beware

If you are sending photos by Bluetooth, the other device must be paired with your phone, have Bluetooth turned on and accept the request to download the photos when they are sent. When pairing two devices, a password will be created on the first device that then needs to be entered into the second device.

1. Open a photo at full size and tap on the **Share** button

2. Select one of the sharing options. This will be dependent on the apps on your phone, but should include email, messaging, and online storage options such as **Google Drive**

Sharing with Bluetooth

To share with another device using Bluetooth:

1. Access a photo or make a selection of photos (as shown in Step 4 on page 162), tap on the **Share** button, and then the **Bluetooth** option, from the **More** button in Step 2 above

2. If your Bluetooth is not on, turn it **On** in the **Settings** app

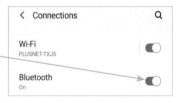

3. Select the device with which you want to share your photo(s). These will be sent wirelessly via Bluetooth

(11) Online with Chrome

This chapter looks at browser options on Android and also viewing all of your favorite websites with the Chrome browser.

Android Web Browsers

Web browsing is an essential part of our digital world, and on Android phones this functionality can be provided by a variety of web browsers customized for this purpose. They can usually display websites in two ways:

- Optimized for viewing on mobile devices, which are versions that are designed specifically for viewing in this format.

- Full versions of websites (rather than the mobile versions), which are the same as those used on a desktop computer.

Different Android phones have different default browsers but they all have the same general functionality:

- Viewing web pages.

- Bookmarking pages.

- Tabbed browsing – i.e. using tabs to view more than one web page within the same browser window.

If you do not want to use the default browser that is provided with your phone, there is a range of browsers that can be downloaded, for free, from the Play Store.

Don't forget

Mobile versions of a website usually have **m.** before the rest of the website address – e.g. **m.mysite.com**

Enter **browsers for android** into the **Play Store Search box** to view the available options.

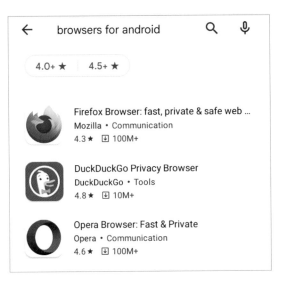

Opening Pages

Web pages can be opened on a phone in an almost identical way as on a desktop computer or laptop. Some Android web browsers display a list of top sites when you open a browser or create a new tab. (The examples on the following pages are for the **Chrome** browser but other browsers operate in a similar way.)

The Chrome browser can be downloaded from the Play Store if it is not already on your phone. This is a Google product and integrates closely with other Google apps on your phone.

1 The **Search/Address** box can be used to search for keywords or phrases, or you can use it to find specific web pages and sites. Enter text into the **Search/Address** box. If a web address is displayed, tap on it to go directly to that website

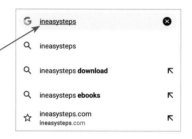

2 Tap on the Search icon next to search for the item on the web. Tap on an item in the **Search/Address** box to view it

3 For a web address – e.g. one that ends in .com – the web page will be opened; if you have just entered a keyword in the Search/Address box, then the results page will be opened for that keyword. Tap one of the links as required

Swipe outward with your thumb and forefinger on a web page to zoom in on it; pinch inward to zoom back out. You can double-tap with one finger to zoom in and out too, but this zooms in to a lesser degree than swiping.

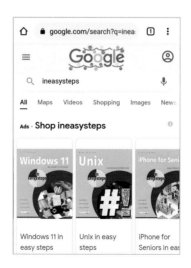

Bookmarking Pages

The favorite web pages that you visit can be bookmarked so that you can find them quickly. To do this:

1 Open the page that you want to bookmark and tap on the **Menu** button at the top of the window

Hot tip

If bookmarks are saved into the **Mobile bookmarks** folder, they will also be available on other mobile devices when you are signed in to your Google Account.

2 Tap on this button to bookmark the page

3 Tap on the button in Step 2 again to edit a bookmark. Tap here in the **Folder** box to specify a folder into which you want to save a bookmark

Don't forget

Tap the **Delete** icon in Step 3 to remove the bookmark.

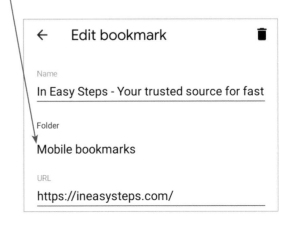

4 Tap on a folder to select it, or tap on the **New folder...** button to create a new folder to use

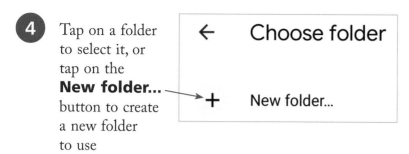

5 Give the folder a name and tap on the check mark symbol to create the folder. Then, tap on the back arrow button to save and return to the previous page

 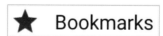

Viewing bookmarks

To view pages that have been bookmarked:

1 To view bookmarks, tap on the **Menu** button and tap on the **Bookmarks** option

The **Menu** button can also be used to open a new tab. See page 173 for more details about using tabs.

★ **Bookmarks**

2 If folders have been created, tap on one to view its contents

3 Tap on a bookmarked page to open the page in the **Chrome** browser

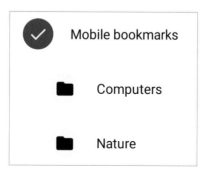

Links and Images

Links and images are both essential items on websites; links provide the functionality for moving between pages and sites, while images provide the all-important graphical element. To work with these:

172

1 Tap and hold on a link to access its options (tap once on a link to go directly to the linked page). The options include opening the link in a new tab, opening it in a new tab that does not get recorded by the browser's history (**Open in Incognito tab**), copying the web address or link text so that it can be shared with someone or pasted into a document, and downloading the link so that it can be viewed offline

2 Tap and hold on an image to access its options. The options include viewing it on its own (**Open image in new tab**), downloading it, searching Google for the image, or sharing the image

Open image in new tab

Preview image

Copy image

Download image

Search image with Google Lens New

Share image

Using Tabs

Tabs are a common feature on web browsers and allow you to open numerous pages within the same browser window. To do this on an Android phone:

1 Tap on this button in the top right-hand corner of the browser window to view current tabs

The button in Step 1 displays the number of tabs currently open within the **Chrome** browser.

2 Tap on this button to add a new tab

3 Open a new page from the **Search or type web address** box, or any bookmarked pages that are displayed

If there are a lot of tabs open, swipe up and down in the tabs window to view them.

4 Tap on the tab button in Step 1 to view all tabs. Tap on a page to open it. Press and hold on the top of a page and drag it into a different position on the tabs screen

Being Incognito

If you do not want a record to be kept of the web pages that you have visited, most browsers have a function where you can view pages "in private" so that the details are not stored by the browser. In Chrome, this is performed with the **Incognito** function.

If the **Incognito** option is used, web pages will not be stored in the browser history or the search history.

If children are using your phone, you may not know what they are looking at on the web if they use the **Incognito** option.

1 Tap on the **Menu** button and tap on the **New Incognito tab** option

⊕ New tab

New Incognito tab

⋮

2 The Incognito page opens in a new tab, but any other open tabs are not visible (unless they are incognito too). Open a web page in the same way as for a standard tab

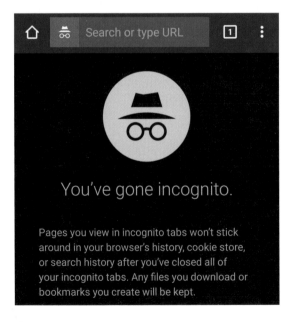

3 Incognito pages are denoted by this icon in the top left-hand corner of the browser

174

Browser Settings

Mobile browsers have the usual range of settings that can be accessed from the **Menu** button.

1 Tap on the **Menu** button and tap on the **Settings** option

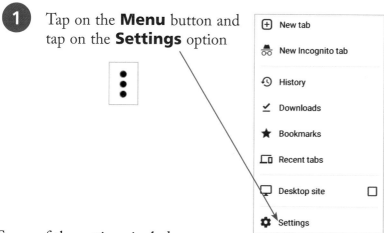

Some of the settings include:

- **Search engine**. This can be used to set a default search engine for the browser.

- **Passwords**. Use this to make selections for how passwords are dealt with by the browser.

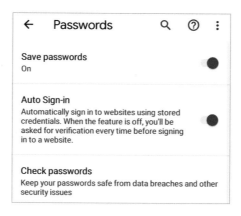

Beware

If other people are going to be using your account on your phone, do not turn on the **Auto Sign-in** option for websites in the **Passwords** section.

...cont'd

- Under the **Advanced** heading, tap on the **Privacy and security** option to specify how your browsing data is used.

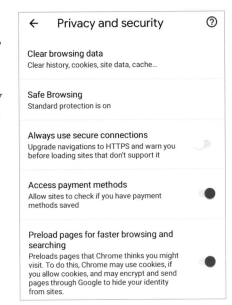

← Privacy and security ⑦

Clear browsing data
Clear history, cookies, site data, cache...

Safe Browsing
Standard protection is on

Always use secure connections
Upgrade navigations to HTTPS and warn you
before loading sites that don't support it

Access payment methods
Allow sites to check if you have payment
methods saved

Preload pages for faster browsing and
searching
Preloads pages that Chrome thinks you might
visit. To do this, Chrome may use cookies, if
you allow cookies, and may encrypt and send
pages through Google to hide your identity
from sites.

- Under the **Advanced** heading, tap on the **Accessibility** option to specify the text size for viewing web pages.

Don't forget

A cookie is a small piece of data that is stored by the browser, containing information about websites that have been visited.

- Under the **Advanced** heading, tap on the **Site settings** option. Select each option in turn, and then check on or off the options for cookies, JavaScript (which is required to give you full functionality of most websites), and pop-up menus. Tap on the **Location** option to specify whether other websites can use your current location, and the **All sites** option to view settings for individual websites.

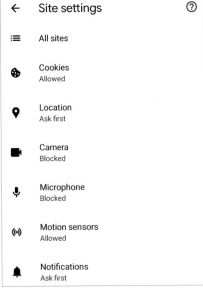

← Site settings ⑦

≣ All sites

🍪 Cookies
Allowed

📍 Location
Ask first

📷 Camera
Blocked

🎤 Microphone
Blocked

((•)) Motion sensors
Allowed

🔔 Notifications
Ask first

12 Staying Secure

This chapter looks at security and privacy issues and your overall digital wellbeing.

Beware

The world of viruses is a fast-moving one, so it is a good idea to keep up-to-date with the latest viruses that are around. Periodically, search Google for "latest Android viruses" to see what is currently out there.

Don't forget

If young children or grandchildren are borrowing your phone for tasks such as surfing the web or playing games, discuss any restrictions that you have put in place so that they can learn about issues covering online safety.

Security Issues

Security is a significant issue for all forms of computing, and this is no different for Android phone users. Three of the main areas of concern are:

- **Getting viruses from apps**. Android apps can contain viruses like any other computer programs, but there are antivirus apps that can be used to try to detect viruses. Unlike programs on computers or laptops with  file management systems, apps on a phone tend to be more self-contained and do not interact with the rest of the system. This means that if they do contain viruses it is less likely that they will infect the whole phone.

- **Losing your phone or having it stolen**. If your phone is lost or stolen you will want to try to get it back and also lock it remotely so that no-one else can gain access to your data and content. The Android Settings page has an option for finding a lost phone (see page 186), and some antivirus apps also have this option.

- **Restricting access for children**. If you have young children or grandchildren who are using your phone, you will want to know what they are using it for. This is particularly important for the web, social media sites, video-sharing sites and 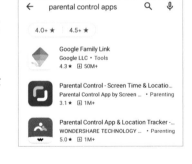 messaging sites where there is the potential to interact with other people. There is also a range of parental control apps that can be downloaded from the Play Store. These can be used to limit access to certain types of apps or content.

About Antivirus Apps

Android phones are certainly not immune from viruses and malware, and the FBI's Internet Crime Complaint Center (IC3) has even published advice and information about malicious software aimed at Android users. Some general precautions that can be taken to protect your phone are:

- Use an antivirus app on your phone. There are several of these, and they can scan your phone for any existing viruses and also check new apps and email attachments for potential problems.

- Apps that are provided in the Play Store are checked for viruses before they are published, but if you are in any doubt about an app, research it online before you download it. If you do an online search for an app, any issues related to it should be available.

- Do not download any email attachments if you are not sure of their authenticity. If you do not know the person who has sent the email, then delete it.

Functionality of antivirus apps

There are several antivirus apps available in the Play Store. Search for **android antivirus apps** (or similar) to view the apps. Most security apps have a similar range of features:

- **Scanning** for viruses and malicious software (malware).

- **Online protection** against malicious software on websites.

- **Anti-theft protection**. This can be used to lock your phone, locate it through **Location Services**, wipe its contents if they are particularly sensitive, and instruct it to let out an alert sound.

For some of the functions of antivirus and security apps, a sign-in is required.

A lot of antivirus and security apps are free, but there is usually a Pro or Premium version that has to be paid for. It is worth downloading several of the free versions of antivirus apps to see how you like them and to try out the different functions that they have.

Some antivirus apps also have an option for backing up items such as your contacts, which can then be restored to your phone or another device if they are deleted or corrupted at all.

Privacy

Privacy, and how your personal data is used, is of increasing importance in the digital world. With Android phones using Android 10, there are a number of privacy settings that can be applied to ensure that you have as much control as possible over your data. To use these:

The **Privacy** options have been updated in Android 10.

1 Tap on the **Settings** app

2 Tap on the **Privacy** tab

> Privacy
> Permission manager

3 Tap on the **Permission manager** option to specify options for how apps are allowed to interact with one another, and access the data within them

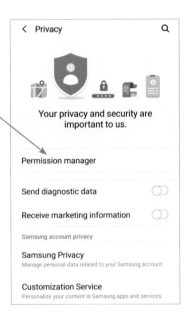

4 Swipe down the screen to access further privacy options; see the next page

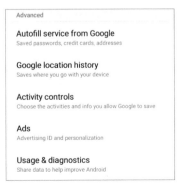

5 Tap on the **Autofill service from Google** option in Step 4 on the previous page to specify which items can have passwords added automatically – i.e. the password is remembered from when it is initially entered

| ← Autofill with Google |
| Use Autofill with Google ⬤ |
| 🧑 Account
nickvandome@googlemail.com |
| ⓘ Personal information |
| 📍 Addresses |
| 💳 Payment methods |
| 🔑 Passwords |

6 Tap on the **Google location history** option in Step 4 to turn this function **On** or **Off** so that your location is tracked, or not, depending on where you are

Location History

Saves where you go with your devices, even when you aren't using a specific Google service, to give you personalized maps, recommendations based on places you've visited, and more. Learn more

⊘ On   Turn off

7 Tap on the **Activity controls** option in Step 4 to specify how your web browsing is saved, or not

Web & App Activity

Saves your activity on Google sites and apps, including associated info like location, to give you faster searches, better recommendations, and more personalized experiences in Maps, Search, and other Google services. Learn more

⊘ On   Turn off

8 Tap on the **Ads** option in Step 4 to specify how you are targeted by online adverts

9 Tap on the **Usage & diagnostics** option in Step 4 to drag the button **On** or **Off** to allow or deny usage data from your phone to be shared with Google

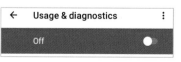

Location History can be a useful option for apps such as **Google Maps**, which can improve its service based on your location.

Digital Wellbeing

As we all spend more time on our digital devices, there is an increasing awareness of the need to keep control of our usage and ensure that we do not spend too long staring at screens. With Android 10, this can be done with the **Digital Wellbeing** settings, which allow you to track, and limit, your screen time. To use these:

The **Digital Wellbeing** settings are a new feature in Android 10.

1 Tap on the **Settings** app

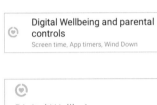

2 Tap on the **Digital Wellbeing and parental controls** tab

> Digital Wellbeing and parental controls
> Screen time, App timers, Wind Down

3 Tap on the **Digital Wellbeing** option

> Digital Wellbeing
> Use app timers and other tools to keep track of your screen time and unplug more easily.
> →

4 Details of your current screen time usage are displayed, including apps that have been used

5 Tap on the **Screen time** button to set a goal for how much screen time to use

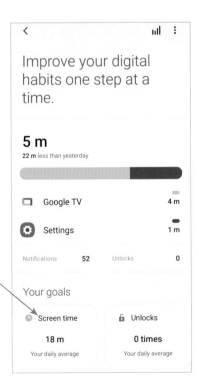

6 Scroll up the screen to view the full range of **Digital Wellbeing** options

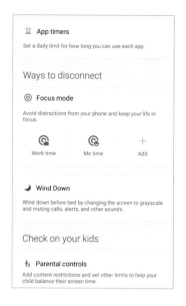

7 Tap on the **App timers** button in Step 6 to set time limits for specific apps

8 Tap on the **No timer** button next to an app to set a time limit for it

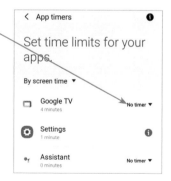

App time limits can be overridden once they are reached, so it still requires a certain amount of willpower to not use your apps too much.

9 Select a time limit for the app, or tap on the **Custom** button to select a specific time period

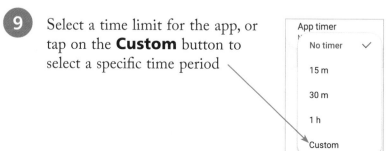

...cont'd

Hot tip

Turn off your Android phone before you go to bed so that you can relax properly and hopefully get a better night's sleep.

10 Tap on the **Focus mode** button in Step 6 on page 183 to set times for not being interrupted

◎ Focus mode

Avoid distractions from your phone and keep your life in focus.

Work time   Me time   Add

11 Tap on the **Start** button to set up the required Focus mode, which enables you to specify certain apps that are available so that you are not distracted by notifications or alerts from all of the apps on your Android phone

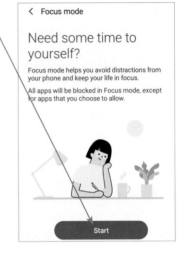

‹ Focus mode

Need some time to yourself?

Focus mode helps you avoid distractions from your phone and keep your life in focus.

All apps will be blocked in Focus mode, except for apps that you choose to allow.

Start

12 Tap on the **Wind Down** button in Step 6 on page 183 to set relaxation options

☾ Wind Down

Wind down before bed by changing the screen to grayscale and muting calls, alerts, and other sounds.

13 Drag the **Turn on as scheduled** button **On** to specify a time period for when the screen color is turned to grayscale, to aid relaxation and sleep, and mute calls and phone sounds

‹ Wind Down

Wind down before bed by changing the screen to grayscale and muting calls, alerts, and other sounds.

Turn on as scheduled
Sun, Mon, Tue, Wed, Thu, Fri, Sat
22:00 - 07:00 the next day

14 Tap on the **Parental controls** button

Parental controls
Add content restrictions and set other limits to help your child balance their screen time.

in Step 6 on page 183 to set limits for children or grandchildren if they are using your Android phone

If you are setting parental controls for grandchildren, make sure that you tell them what you have done, and why, so that they fully understand why certain options may not be available.

15 Tap on the **Next** button to create parental controls for someone else using your phone

Next steps
Set up parental controls for your child

Link your child's Google Account with your own in a Google family group

Choose apps for this device & set filters

From your own device, set controls like bedtime & screen time limits

Next

16 Tap on the **Get started** button to complete a step-by-step process for setting up parental controls

Set up parental controls
with Google's Family Link

Supervise this phone remotely with the Family Link app for parents

Keep an eye on screen time and set limits as needed

Add restrictions to Google services, like app approvals or content filters on Google Play

Get started

17 This includes adding the email address of the other person who is using the phone so that you can add restrictions in terms of screen time and the apps that are available to them. Click **Next** to complete the process

Google
Parent account
to continue to Family Link

Enter the Google Account you'll use to supervise your child.

Email or phone

Forgot email?

Before using this app, you can review Family Link's privacy policy and terms of service.

Next

185

Locating Your Phone

If you lose your phone or it is stolen, you can try to find its location via the **Find My Mobile** option.

Don't forget

A lost phone has to be turned on and **Location** enabled in **Settings** > **Location** for it to be located via the **Find My Mobile** feature.

Don't forget

Depending on the type of Android phone you are using, you may need to link it to an account belonging to your phone's manufacturer as part of the initial process for activating **Find My Mobile**.

Hot tip

The Google website can also be used to find a lost phone, using your Google Account. This can be set up via **Settings** > **Google** > **Find My Device**.

1 Access **Settings** > **Biometrics and security**

2 Drag the **Find My Mobile** button **On**

| Find My Mobile | |
| On without Remote unlock | 🔵 |

3 Your phone can be tracked from the website of your Android manufacturer. Select options for the functionality of the **Find My Mobile** function, such as: being able to remotely lock your phone if it is lost or stolen; enabling your phone to send its last known location to the Find My Mobile server; and enabling your phone to be found even if it is offline

Index

D

E

F

G

Q

R

S